D0765402

COMPARATIVE CRIMINOLOGY

Volume 31
SAGE RESEARCH PROGRESS SERIES IN CRIMINOLOGY

SAGE RESEARCH PROGRESS SERIES IN CRIMINOLOGY

Published in Cooperation with the American Society of Criminology

Series Editor: **MICHAEL R. GOTTFREDSON,** *State University of New York at Albany*

Founding Series Editor: **JAMES A. INCIARDI,** *University of Delaware*

SAGE RESEARCH PROGRESS SERIES IN CRIMINOLOGY
VOLUME 31

COMPARATIVE CRIMINOLOGY

EDITED BY
Israel L. Barak-Glantz
and Elmer H. Johnson

Published in cooperation with the
AMERICAN SOCIETY OF CRIMINOLOGY

SAGE PUBLICATIONS
Beverly Hills / London / New Delhi

For information address:

SAGE Publications, Inc.
275 South Beverly Drive
Beverly Hills, California 90212

SAGE Publications India Pvt. Ltd.
C-236 Defence Colony
New Delhi 110 024, India

SAGE Publications Ltd
28 Banner Street
London EC1Y 8QE, England

Printed in the United States of America

Library of Congress Cataloging in Publication Data

Main entry under title:

Comparative criminology.

    (Sage research progress series in criminology ; v. 31)
    "Published in cooperation with the American Society of Criminology."
    Includes bibliographies.
    1. Crime and criminals—Congresses. I. Barak-Glantz, Israel L. II. Johnson, Elmer Hubert. III. American Society of Criminology. IV. Series.
HV6025.C585   1983   364   83-17853
ISBN 0-8039-2141-1
FIRST PRINTING

CONTENTS

1

Elmer H. Johnson
Southern Illinois University

Israel L. Barak-Glantz
Wayne State University

INTRODUCTION

Comparative criminology is not merely the cross-cultural comparison of crime rates. Rather, it is a scientific approach and an exercise in macro-analysis whereby the qualities of a given phenomenon or the purposes and meaning of a given activity are seen to be derived from the broad setting in which they are located. Thus it seeks to locate commonalities and differences in patterns of criminality and crime among divergent economic, political, social, or cultural systems. Criminality is one of the classes of social deviance that express the qualities of a particular population, the workings of social institutions in a given social system, the level of socioeconomic development, and the rate of industrial and urban growth. Because criminality is prevalent in both affluent and developing nations where contemporary conditions strain the institutional matrix, there are similarities among socioeconomic and political systems in reactions to criminality. Yet societies have their own histories, characteristics, and perceptions of the significance of criminality. Overgeneralizations are gravely risked when those fundamental differences are not given serious consideration.

This volume comprises papers selected from those presented in sessions organized by the Division on International Criminology, a unit of the American Society of Criminology. Among the many worthy papers presented at the society's annual meeting in 1982 in Toronto, certain ones were chosen that provide coverage of theoretical and empirical aspects of the subject matter of comparative criminology. This specialized field within criminology, Shelley (1981: xix) tells us, "allows research at numerous analytical levels ranging from the individual offense and offender to overall crime trends and criminal justice systems." Specifically, comparative criminological research must be conducted at least on the following three levels: (a) the causes of the process by which a person commits his first offense or a juvenile takes his first step toward delinquency; (b) the problem of recidivism and the process that leads a first offender to become a persistent, professional criminal and ultimately a hardened incorrigible one; and (c) crime on the social level in comparing two or more societies and/or cultures (i.e., the fluctuation of crime rates during a given time, genesis and volume of special types of crimes, and the interrelationships between crime and social change). The range of possible topics is among the sources of the fascination of comparative criminology, but a single, relatively slender volume can offer only a glimpse of that great range.

SOME BENEFITS OF COMPARATIVE CRIMINOLOGY

Comparative studies have a long history in the fields of law, sociology, anthropology, history, linguistics, and political science. Among those credited with early comparative studies are Emile Durkheim, Jeremy Bentham, Gabriel Tarde, Adolph Quetelet, and Alexis de Tocqueville, who made significant contributions to criminology.

The authors of the papers included in this volume provide the opportunity to experience vicariously the benefits of comparative criminology. Since anything affecting human behaviors and institutions is pertinent to criminology, it may be said that criminology is useful as a survey of the total span of knowledge. Because criminal law reflects the fundamental values and concerns of a people, it is one of the most faithful mirrors of a given civilization. In studying the operation of criminal law and the patterns of organized reactions to criminality, courses in criminology are particularly appropriate for inclusion within the liberal arts as well as for the education of those students aspiring to careers in the administration of criminal justice.

Those benefits of criminology are supplemented when transnational examination of criminological phenomena is undertaken. The scholars and researchers of one nation can gain a more profound understanding of the issues that concern them by exchanging their experiences and findings with their counterparts in other nations. Theoretical analyses are strengthened, as Bendix (1963: 535-538) notes, by the probing of problematics of the human condition, by highlighting the contrasts between different human situations and social structures while also underscoring the structural variations.

For the practitioner and policymaker, learning about the criminal and penal policy of other cultures and nations provides an invaluable source of insight and ingenuity in dealing with crime and criminal behavior. Comparative criminological and criminal justice system studies facilitate the unraveling of the relative import of specific sociolegal, political, and economic conditions in the making of policy and practice in criminology. A more complete understanding of these variations may lead to the development of creative methods of handling the problem of crime.

For lay readers, comparative treatments such as those in this volume expand intellectual horizons and cultural appreciation by delineating alternatives to their own perceptions of criminality and to the familiar environments within which reactions to deviance are shaped. The emergence of new nations in Africa has dramatically demonstrated the potentiality of comparative criminology in that respect. Clifford (1983: 87) lends substance to that point in stating:

> It was more and more appreciated that the cultural dimensions of crime and its control had more significance than they had previously been accorded. To explain crime and its control, it was necessary to know as much about the areas of the world that were untroubled with crime as it was to have libraries of publications on the situation in the more developed but crime-ridden areas. If the developing nations had less crime and were likely to get more with modernization and socioeconomic growth, could they not preserve at least some of their advantages by profiting from the mistakes of developed countries?

PROBLEMS FACED BY COMPARATIVE STUDIES

Criminology has not taken sufficient advantage of the potentialities of the comparative method. The great challenges for effective use of the method at least partly explain the insufficiency, but the promise is particularly attractive for criminology. There is a stronger international flavor than for the study of criminal law, Mannheim (1965: 20-21) insists, because it is a non-legal discipline and therefore is more likely to avoid the parochial outlook that has characterized the legal analyses, especially in the past. "Unhampered by the limits of any national legislation," he says, criminology "can afford to tackle its problems in a world-wide spirit." He is correct in noting the greater promise of criminology when it deals with the sociocultural patterns rather than the legal norms that are selective and often distorted interpretations of more general norms and values. It would be an oversimplification, however, to argue that the data of criminology are free of legalistic parochialism.

The serious methodological weaknesses of official statistics for transnational comparisons have been widely discussed. Christie (1970), for example, finds "a great deal of criminological data more useful for the purpose of understanding the system of control than for understanding of what makes people criminal." He suggests that comparative research circumvent official data by studies of actual behavior and undertake examinations of total systems and of cross-national levels of perceived deviance. Clinard (1978: 229) advices that we study legislative concern, theft insurance rates, hospital statistics, and crime victimization rates. Perhaps even more chastening for criminologists is the possibility that theoretical orientations, believed to be suitable for a given society, are still too narrow in scope and too grounded in the conditions of that society to be extrapolated in cross-cultural investigations. Friday (1973: 152) warns: "Criminologists have been plagued by the inability of the discipline to develop any explanations of criminality that could be considered 'universal.' "

Assessment of the prospects for mature comparative criminology must thus include recognition of the need for a sufficient supply of criminologists who are prepared to engage in authentic transnational research. Comparative analysis raises its peculiar methodological, ideological, and communicative problems that call for the very attributes of the scientists that advocates of the comparative method appear to see as products of comparative research (Johnson, 1979: 27). Competence is severely tested by the formidable demands of cross-cultural research outlined by Newman (1977), including equivalence of meanings, response bias, equivalence of interviewers, recruiting appropriately skilled research personnel, temporal equivalence, and drawing of samples.

Further, whether oriented to the social or behavioral sciences, criminologists are vulnerable to the ethnocentrism of accepting the epistemology of the academy of their respective nation and even subconsciously the folklore about crime found among their people. The concepts of a discipline, as shaped by the intellectual history of the given nation, lend direction to inquiry, but they also screen the perception of reality. The comparative criminologist has reason to be particularly aware of questions raised about the value objectivity and political neutrality of scientists and the justice system.

Piers Beirne's chapter concentrates on relativism as the hidden reef that threatens to destroy the theoretical soundness of comparative investigations. In the 1970s, he says, comparative criminology experienced unprecedented stimulus for a number of reasons. After a searching review of comparative studies, Bierne distinguishes three methodologies: the method of agreement, the method of difference, and methodological relativism. To guide comparative criminologists, he provides some rules for formulating cross-cultural generalizations about crime.

ECONOMIC CRIMES IN COMMUNIST NATIONS

Ideological conflicts between political systems are a major stimulus to comparative ethnocentrism and to the raising of barriers to the easy and open communication among scientists. When "cold war" ideologies infiltrate explanations for criminality, the profundity and reliability of criminological analyses are jeopardized. When prejudgements are suspended and attention riveted on the similarities and differences between capitalist and communist states, there is rich opportunity to identify the fundamentals of criminological phenomena and to test propositions that are claimed to be universal.

In her examination of the control of economic crimes and corruption in the Soviet Union and Poland, Maria Loś deals with the state's use of criminal penalties to manage "crimes against the central plan," "crimes against communist property relations," and "crimes against communist distribution of good." That feature of criminalization in communist countries is a reflection of their economic system that lacks the profit orientation, market laws, and labor negotiations of capitalist economic systems. Loś describes a centrally planned economy that does not hold the full commitment of the workers, that suffers from the effects of pathological bureaucracy that treats administrative fictions as truths regardless of departures from reality, and that encourages official corruption through system-induced falsifications. State ownership is officially described as "social" or "public" ownership, to suggest popular participation in management of the economy, but Loś finds the regime engaged in political domination that workers resist through "crimes against the central plan" and "crimes against property relations." The scarcity of commodities has given subterranean functions to private middlemen and speculators that are officially defined as criminal.

The analysis invites further comparison of the system-induced criminal behaviors in capitalist economies with those of socialist economies. Examination of white-collar or corporate crimes takes on a freshness when considered in reference to the Loś analysis. Subcultural theories and Merton's anomie theory convey the theme of system-induced strain that invites application to the alienation of segments of the Russian and Polish populations from the political regimes. The labeling, or societal reaction, perspective can be applied with intellectual profit.

MEDIATION IN
THE PEOPLE'S REPUBLIC OF CHINA

The People's Republic of China, the other major communist world power, has been sending signals that it welcomes contacts with the West that serve the development of its backward economy. A pragmatic leadership has embarked on a comprehensive program, called the "Four Modernizations," of long-term industrial, agricultural, military, and scientific-technological development. It would be premature to claim that comparative studies of genuine merit are in immediate prospect, but American criminologists have had unprecedented opportunities to experience directly facets of a criminal justice system previously veiled from foreign observation.

That socialist nation represents a peculiar combination of persistent tradition and contemporary dynamism, strongly colored by the historical experience of its people. Only one of the sources of the expression of a will for independence from foreign influence, Maoism has politicized the criminal justice system in a style that demands understanding of the macro-social control system before one can make sense out of activities that appear at first glance to resemble the administrative patterns of criminal justice in the West.

Among the fascinating opportunities for comparative investigations, Elmer H. Johnson introduces the topic of mediation in the PRC as grounded in the Maoist ideology that would mobilize the masses by raising their political consciousness. This strategy in a "nation without lawyers" invites inspection by reformers of the West who would substitute other forms of dispute settlement for adjudication and criminalization. The popular participation of amateurs in mediation may appear to be an example of grass-roots democracy. Yet comparative criminologists have learned that a criminal justice process must be examined within its particular sociocultural and political milieu. In his preliminary report, Johnson places Chinese mediation within the context of the Maoist ideology in seeking clues to its rationale, purposes, and implementation.

CIVIL VIOLENCE IN TWO SETTINGS

Park (1967: 226) says that "collective behavior is the behavior of individuals under the influence of an impulse that is common and collective, an impulse, in other words, that is the result of social interaction." Collective behavior is intermediary between socially structured roles and completely individualistic behavior, as illustrated by crowds and mobs. Park associated collective behavior with social unrest, in that manifestation of discontent is transmitted among individuals to break up established routines and to produce something akin to the milling of a herd.

Civil violence falls outside the sphere of common crimes some social scientists might prefer to specify as the proper subject matter of criminology, but criminological interest in social control extends beyond those narrow boundaries. Collective behavior is extrainstitutional and therefore appears at first glance to be merely individualistic behavior outside the span of social control. But, as specified above, the occurrence of collective behavior outside of institutionalized roles does not spell the absence of social influence.

In finding similarities and differences between urban riots in Miami and Liverpool, Philip Jenkins and Fred Hutchings place these events within the scope of comparative criminology. Of course, Britain and the United States share many sociocultural and political characteristics, but the literature of the social sciences frequently conveys the message that American culture is particularly prone to violence and that British culture is not. Nevertheless, Jenkins and Hutchings find significant parallels in racial resentments associated with high unemployment, a perceived threat from right-wing terrorism, and a perception of a justice-system's bias against the poor. Differing from the Miami riot, the Liverpool violence was characterized by little ethnic hostility and more by a sense of class rivalry. In tracing the social, economic, and political roots of civil disorders, Jenkins and Hutchings join our other contributors in emphasizing the peculiarities of the contexts of each of the societies being compared.

WOMEN'S RIGHTS AND FEMALE CRIMINALITY

Among the sectors of remarkable changes in recent decades has been the changes in female roles and perceptions of the criminality among women. The cross-cultural perspective is especially pertinent because the status of women varies radically from nation to nation and because the possible relationships between women's status and criminality also vary. A major hypothesis in the American literature is that increased crime rates among women may be explained by female emancipation, in that the differences among the sexes in levels of crime diminish as women gain greater equality of rights and privileges.

It is appropriate that Ineke Haen Marshall selected the Netherlands for cross-cultural testing of that same hypothesis. That country has been credited with great reluctance to impose imprisonment and, when doing so, to exact definitely shorter periods of confinement. The Dutch have a reputation for cultural tolerance and a willingness to trust one another.

Nevertheless, Marshall finds the emancipation hypothesis without support. The Dutch feminists are largely well-educated middle- and upper-class women who are unlikely candidates for criminal justice processing. The legal foundations for emancipation lagged behind those in the United States. Dutch women continue to be family oriented and usually not susceptible to the feminist movement. In the years 1958-1977, female arrests for personal violent crimes, fraud, and embezzlement decreased but increased for crimes against public order and authority, vandalism, and simple theft. Contrary to the emancipation hypothesis, the relative gap between male and female arrests increased for "masculine crimes" in the time period. Property offenses gave greater but still uncertain support to the hypothesis.

APPLIED SIDE OF COMPARATIVE CRIMINOLOGY

The American Society of Criminology describes itself as a body consisting of

> persons interested in the advancement of criminology, including scholarly, scientific and professional knowledge of the etiology, prevention, control, and treatment of crime and delinquency, the measurement and detection of crime, legislation, and the practice of criminal law, the law enforcement, judicial, and corrections systems.

As a component of ASC, the Division on International Criminology also has recognized the importance of applied empirical research on international issues, and of placing such suitable papers on the ASC annual program. This book has been organized appropriately to include also comparative studies emphasizing law enforcement, the courts, and corrections.

Comparative analyses of law enforcement issues are in short supply among the specialized fields of empirical criminology. Knowlton Johnson draws on his research to contribute to the literature on the recruitment of police manpower. Urbanization and the rising demand for responsive and responsible policing have given unprecedented attention to the quality of performance. The selection practices for police personnel are of prime importance to that quality. The status revolution has added to an already complex selection system the issue of recruitment of women and members of minority groups.

In an analysis of selection practices in the United States and Canada, Johnson delineates major methods used in filtering candidates for police work. He further assesses the criticisms directed against the various methods and their implementation, and surveys the changes being made in the selection procedures. Among the differences between the two countries were the following: A large proportion of Canadian departments permit a candidate to fail a stage in the selection process without being removed from consideration; written tests are more likely to be the first stage in the United States; Canada is more likely to place oral interviews first in the sequence; few Canadians used the polygraph; and litigation against selection methods is less likely in Canada.

PARTICIPATION IN COURTS: LAY JUDGES AND JURORS

The administration of the law depends ultimately on the legitimacy of its outcomes as perceived by the public. Reformers often advocate that laypersons be deliberately involved in court proceedings as a means of furthering legitimacy. In the United States, volunteers have been recruited to participate in activities of courts through performance of administrative duties, probation work, or as "court watchers" who observe and report on the effectiveness of particular courts. Nancy T. Wolfe deals with two other strategies: jurors and lay judges.

In implementing a comparison of data drawn from West Germany and the United States, Wolfe examines American petit jurors and German lay judges in regard to public participation. Her chapter concentrates on the length of service and method of assignment because they are crucial factors in Americans' reluctance to serve as jurors. She delineates the differences in the policies and procedures of the two countries.

The American petit jury and the West German lay judiciary are the primary examples of public participation in the respective countries. Wolfe is unable to compare each strategy directly because each is not found in the other country. Thereby, her paper illustrates the necessity for improvisation by comparative criminologists who pursue a key issue (lay participation in this instance) in fundamentally distinctive legal systems.

PRISON GUARDS IN
SCANDINAVIA AND AMERICA

Unlike the long-term interest in the experiences and problems of prisoners, serious research attention to those of their keepers has been given only in the last decade in the United States. Correctional officers are in most continuous relationships with inmates and yet "fraternization" is prohibited. Unlike the public acceptance of custodial duties in a positive way, the guarding of prisoners has come to be seen as disreputable "dirty work." Correctional officers typically see themselves as a minority group suffering unwarranted stigmatization and the stresses of dangerous work without the authentic support of their superiors.

Peter Wickman's chapter is a worthy addition to a growing literature because of three unique features. First, he draws on the insightful literature on the sociology of organizations to give theoretical thrust to what has been published on the social structure of prisons. Second, he focuses his analysis on the aggravation of stress for the keepers by the prison social structure. He proposes a model for delineating the prison organization inducement of stress among correctional officers. Third, he draws data from Finland, Sweden, and Denmark for the purpose of transnational comparison.

PROSPECTS FOR COMPARATIVE CRIMINOLOGY

In their respective ways, the authors of the chapters in this book have demonstrated the breadth of topics that fall within the scope of comparative criminology. They have endeavored to cope with the conceptual and methodological difficulties raised by the diverse sociocultural settings in which the selected issues are found. The level of success achieved is a tribute to their ingenuity.

For many decades there have been expressions of faith in the potentialities and necessity for comparative studies in criminology, but accomplishments have not matched these hopes. The contributors to this book have fashioned their papers without collaboration. It is significant that we, the editors, were able to relate these papers to produce a reasonably integrated volume. That significance lies in the widespread recognition that the macrosystems of societies and the microsystems of criminal justice must be studied—not just the persons treated as criminals—if criminal behavior is to be understood and if criminal policies and practices are to benefit from more profound understanding. For those ends, comparative criminology has a place and function.

REFERENCES

BENDIX, R. (1963) "Concepts and generalizations in comparative sociological studies." American Sociological Review 28: 532-539.

CHRISTIE, N. (1970) "Comparative criminology." Canadian Journal of Corrections 12: 40-46.

CLIFFORD, W. (1983) "Criminology in developing nations—African and Asian examples," in E. H. Johnson (ed.) International Handbook of Contemporary Developments in Criminology, Volume I: General Issues and the Americas, Westport, CT: Greenwood Press.

CLINARD, M. B. (1978) "Comparative crime victimization surveys: some problems and results." International Journal of Criminology and Penology 6: 221-231.

FRIDAY, P. C. (1973) "Problems in comparative criminology: comments on the feasibility and implications of research." International Journal of Criminology and Penology 1: 151-160.

JOHNSON, E. H. (1979) "Institutionalization of criminology: a prerequisite to comparative criminology." International Journal of Comparative and Applied Criminal Justice 3: 27-33.

MANNHEIM, H. (1965) Comparative Criminology. Boston: Houghton Mifflin.

NEWMAN, G. R. (1977) "Problems of method in comparative criminology." International Journal of Comparative and Applied Criminal Justice 1: 17-31.

PARK, R. E. (1967) On Social Control and Collective Behavior. Chicago: University of Chicago Press.

SHELLEY, L. I. (1981) Readings in Comparative Criminology. Carbondale: Southern Illinois University Press.

2

Piers Beirne

University of Southern Maine

GENERALIZATION AND ITS DISCONTENTS
The Comparative Study of Crime

To compare the "willingness in obedience" to law of an Australian savage with a New Yorker, or of a Melanesian with a Nonconformist citizen of Glasgow, is indeed a perilous proceeding [Bronislaw Malinowski, *Crime and Custom in Savage Society*].

More than fifty years have elapsed since Malinowski voiced this celebrated warning directed to those who in the 1920s unquestioningly inserted comparative material into the conceptual schema of Durkheim and Maine. Time and the fickle landscape of theories and theorists have not dulled its importance; theoretical dogmatism, especially in the context of comparative analysis, is usually tantamount to cultural imperialism.

The present essay was written during a veritable explosion of interest among American criminologists in the etiology of crime in other cultures. The remarks that follow, crudely brief and thematic as they are, should be understood as a polemic against many of the recent studies.

THE RISE OF COMPARATIVE CRIMINOLOGY

To the erstwhile historian of intellectual ideas, the origin of comparative criminology harbors something of a mystery. As a disciplined inquiry, it seems clear that comparative criminology emerged no earlier

AUTHOR'S NOTE: I wish to thank Susan Corrente Beirne for her comments on the first draft of this chapter, and Rosy Miller for preparing it for publication.

than the first quarter of the twentieth century. But its history can putatively be traced, it can be argued, to the rationalist agenda of the Enlightenment in the late eighteenth century. Hegel, Montesquieu, Bentham, and Adam Smith were among many Enlightenment authors who discussed aspects of crime, and criminal law, in cultures other than their own. But the *angst* of Nietzschean great men do not constitute the proper hallmarks of a discipline. No Enlightenment authors pursued the comparative study of crime — the systematic comparison of crime in two or more cultures — as a coherent enterprise. Their discussions of crime were mainly illustrative of, and therefore secondary to, prior objects specified by disciplines as diverse as jurisprudence, social philosophy, theology and architecture. Perhaps the conceptual history of comparative criminology is better traced to Emile Durkheim and his abiding concern with moral education, crime, and the conditions of social order in France? Familiarity, too, can breed content. One could additionally refer to the evolutionary dogma of Darwin and Sir Henry Maine and to the statistical skills of Quetelet, Guerry, and Tarde. It is hard not to be impressed, moreover, by the wealth of comparative material found in books such as Ferri's *Criminal Sociology,* Lombroso's *Crime: Its Causes and Remedies,* and Tarde's *La Criminalité Comparée.*

Such putative and would-be histories — doubtless one day to be written on an expanded scale — fail to discover the embryonic intentions of present criminologists in those of the distant past. None of the above authors undertook the comparative study of crime with the rigorous methods and sensitive concepts required of cross-cultural analysis. Their raw material of study typically extended their national chauvinism to other cultures, places and times. Tarde's promising *La Criminalité Comparée* (1902) exemplifies the genre of this period and typically disappoints; its four short chapters (the criminal type, criminal statistics, penal problems, and problems of criminality) do little more than selectively apply French positivism and Lombrosian atavism to Europe, barbarism, and the Homeric myths. Comparative criminology, I suggest, has no disciplinary history. Such a history cannot be discovered, or invented, in the comparative musings ("ye beastly devices of ye heathen") of Enlightenment or nineteenth-century figures. It cannot be found in the small yet flourishing school of legal anthropology in the 1930s and 1940s, and it properly appears nowhere in modern American criminology itself. The intellectual history of a discipline must be composed of more than lengthy silences broken only by the occasional indulgences of great men.

No research program in comparative criminology existed even as late as the 1950s and 1960s. Marsh (1967: 449-453) has recorded that from 1950 to 1963 only a tiny fraction of journal articles in sociology, social anthropology, and social psychology was addressed to the broad area of conformity and deviance. Of this fraction, only a minority systematically compared the phenomena of crime in two or more cultures. Criminologists rarely ventured far from home during this Cold War period. When they did engage in foreign research they tended to do so in the accessible countries of Western Europe. Even the limited attention given to non-Western cultures has itself been highly selective; attention has tended to focus on a few cultures, namely, India, China, Japan, Israel, South Africa, and the U.S.S.R.[1] More surprising, perhaps, is the long silence among "radical" criminologists about crime in the underdeveloped world and about imperialist crimes against that world. Abstract exegeses on socialism and the withering away of law and crime, Stalinist proclamations that crime is caused by bourgeois morality, abstract exegeses about socialism and the withering away of law, and the like—these trivial slogans ignore the difficulties of cross-cultural comparison altogether.

It is instructive to reread the major comparative texts of the 1960s. Mannheim's *Comparative Criminology* (1965) follows Tarde in borrowing extensively from cultures around the globe, but its erudite pages nowhere explore systematic cross-cultural analysis. Comparativism must be distinguished from eclecticism. Wolfgang and Ferracuti's *The Subculture of Violence* (1965) is commonly regarded (Mannheim 1965: xi; Clinard and Abbott 1973: 3) as comparative, but of its 400 pages only 3 involve the systematic comparison of two or more cultures. Another 9 pages are insular descriptions of aggressive subcultures in seven countries. Cavan and Cavan's *Delinquency and Crime: Cross-Cultural Perspectives* (1968) treats each of 14 societies separately; its cross-cultural analysis is limited to introductory and concluding remarks. All three texts, therefore, primarily comprise single culture studies. But single-culture studies—"we do it this way, they do it that way"—provide, at best additively, only the preparatory spirit of cross-cultural investigation.

These silences are all the more surprising given the repeated gestures of approval toward Durkheim's dictum that "comparative sociology is not a particular branch of sociology, it is sociology itself" (1938: 139). But Durkheim's dictum, it should be noted, tells us nothing about how to do comparative research; it simply inveighs that the comparative dimension is an integral part of sociology. From this cryptic and trite injunction any intellectual adventure abroad can be construed as comparative. This could include (as it now does) the export of American models of crime control to any country whose government has resources, human or financial, to waste, but comparative criminology must be firmly distinguished from the simple extension of the tenets of any national criminology to other cultures. The protocols of disciplined, cross-cultural research differ from those of the intracultural analysis of our own culture.

Some of these silences and cultural biases may now be rapidly disappearing. With a pace that accelerated after the publication of Clinard and Abbott's *Crime in Developing Countries* (1973), cross-cultural studies have begun to occupy a distinct and self-assertive place in American criminology in the last few years. Disciplinary progress is evident in the increasing number of criminology monographs with an explicit comparative focus: Lopez-Rey (1970), Black (1976, passim), Newman (1976), Gurr et al. (1977), Clinard (1978), and Shelley (1981a). Few of these works are of the same quality as recent studies in anthropology or comparative history, for example, but overall they are a tremendous advance. Comparative criminology now has several review essays: Chang (1976b: 3-137), Newman and Ferracuti (1980), Friday (1980), Miracle (1981), Cohen (1982), and Sumner (1982b: 1-39). There are discussions of cross-cultural conceptual problems: Christie (1970), Friday (1973), Newman (1975, 1977), Szabo (1975), Janeksela (1977), Vetere and Newman (1977), Sebba (1979), Bennett (1980), Wilkins (1980), and Beirne (1983). This literature has been supplemented with several readers — often the sign of an emerging discipline — that chiefly consist of new work: Chang (1976a), Newman (1980), Cole et al. (1981), Shelley (1981b), and Sumner (1982a). Finally, several contributions to comparative criminology have been made by geographers and anthropologists. The point at which the anthropology and sociology of law intersect, in the massive and complicated area of dispute processing and informal justice, is a fund of information and insight as yet barely recognized by criminologists. I believe this area will eventually prove to be the catalyst for systematic cross-cultural research that is now lacking in both the empirical studies and the conceptual apparatus of mainstream criminology.

Elsewhere (Beirne 1983), I have suggested that recent comparative studies of crime should be treated with more caution than optimism. My argument there asserted that this literature has uncritically taken two propositions from Durkheimian empiricism, and that these propositions are, in combination, incompatible for cross-cultural research. The first proposition is that the goal of comparative criminology is the construction of cross-cultural generalizations about criminal behavior. The second proposition is that such generalizations can be constructed apart from the values, motives, and intentions of those agents, or groups of agents, whose behavior is the raw material of study. My focus in that essay was the consequences of cultural imperialism that ignores subjective and cultural variation in the definition and meaning of criminal behavior. Nowhere does the above-mentioned literature offer any generalizations about crime, or about its causes, that have been adequately established by cross-cultural analysis. What, then, should properly be understood as an "adequate" cross-cultural generalization? What procedural rules must cross-cultural generalizations satisfy?

THE THREE METHODS OF COMPARATIVE CRIMINOLOGY

Recent literature provides only the vaguest of procedural rules for constructing cross-cultural generalizations about crime. By general acknowledgment, Clinard and Abbott (1973) made the most authoritative statement about the procedure of comparative criminology:

> The goal of a comparative criminology should be to develop concepts and generalizations at a level that distinguishes between universals applicable to all societies and unique characteristics representative of one or a small set of societies... research should proceed... first in a single culture at one point in time... second, in societies generally alike... and third in completely dissimilar societies [1973: 2].

This oft-quoted statement is an almost verbatim rendition of advice given in Marsh's *Comparative Sociology* (1967: 6-7). Marsh's advice, in turn, is an impossible prescription that tries to combine aspects of Durkheim's *Rules of Sociological Method* with Weberian ideal types. Nowhere does this statement tell us either how to construct a generalization or, having done so, the procedural tests that it must then satisfy. In practice, it only advises us about the geographical range across which a generalization ultimately must be tested. By what criteria should we identify cultures that are, for example, "completely dissimilar"? Even with such criteria, a third level of verification is unlikely to occur because, as MacIntyre (1971: 266) has argued about comparative political science, the provision of a social environment sufficiently different to make the search for counter-examples interesting will normally be the provision of an environment where we cannot hope to find examples of the original phenomenon. Without such examples, we cannot hope to find counter-examples to it. Such criteria are even more important in a world whose outermost corners have been touched by the flat hand of multinational capital penetration and cultural transfusion. Clinard and Abbott's advice, in fact, suggests a vacuum that begs to be filled with the contents of national chauvinism. Small wonder, then, that two Latin American criminologists (Encinoza and Del Olmo, 1981: 67) have demanded that

> criminological research not be instigated by institutions far from the reality to be studied, since it is likely that the subjects chosen will not correspond to the priorities of that reality, but rather that they will tend to satisfy the canons of the criminological fashion of the moment in developed countries.

To this warning I will soon return. For present purposes, I must stress that even Clinard and Abbott's notion of "a comparative criminology" conflates three very distinct comparative methods in American criminology on which hinges the ability of criminologists to make adequate cross-cultural generalizations. Each method has its peculiar view of how to juxtapose the cases within its scope. One method tries to subsume as many possible cases under some master theory. A second method, informed solely by cases exceptional to the generalizations of the first, is concerned with the unique properties of a given case, and with how that case diverges from all other cases. A third method derives both from relativist rejection of the a priori expectations of the other two, and from the adoption of a "wait and see" attitude to the meaning of action in other cultures. These three methods I term, respectively, the method of agreement, the method of difference, and methodological relativism. Each method has its advantages and costs. Let us briefly examine each in turn by considering representative examples of each.

The Method of Agreement

The primary aim of the method of agreement is to identify a commonality among as many possible empirical cases of crime.[2] Its success is crucially dependent on a criterion for judgments of commonality, or identity, and this is provided by one overarching postulate within a master theory. The more abstract the postulate, the greater the number of empirical cases that will appear to be within its range; each concurring case is intended to convince the reader that the theory is more and more likely to have greater explanatory power than rival theories. Evolutionism, modernization (urbanization-industrialization) and the convergence of modern societies — the postulates of these theories are all sufficiently abstract to operate exclusively with the method of difference.

The best examples of the method of agreement are Clinard and Abbott's *Crime in Developing Countries* Gurr et al.'s *The Politics of Crime and Conflict,* and Shelley's *Crime and Modernization.* Consider Shelley's argument. Shelley's abstract concern is the apparent change in international crime patterns that results from modernization. Her thesis is unusual, in that it combines a master theory with detailed attention to empirical evidence; it states that modernization provides the best theoretical explanation of the evolution of criminality in the last two hundred years. She offers this explanation against a background in which

> most prominent American criminological theories, widely accepted both in the United States and abroad, during the last four decades, are not universal explanations of criminal behavior... [These theories] apply only to the changes that have accompanied the process of modernization... [and] merely explain the dynamics of crime in the present urban environment [1981a: 13].

Contemporary criminologists, her onslaught continues, generalize about the uniqueness of present-day crime problems with little knowledge of historical precedent. However, from the vantage point of the concept of modernization, Shelley asserts, one can evaluate the extent to which development, rather than unique cultural and social characteristics, is responsible for observed changes in criminality.

Shelley establishes her thesis on three fronts. First, she offers an account of the relationships between crime and industrial development. Property crime is the predominant form or urban criminality. Rural areas, with traditionally low crime rates, have relatively high rates of violence and low rates of property crime. Some forms of criminality Shelley claims to be exclusively associated with urban preindustrial society, some with rural preindustrial society. The onset of the industrial revolution transforms the social morphology of crime, with crimes of violence receding and property crimes becoming the hallmark of modernization. Rural migrants, newly arrived in urban centers, are unable to adapt to the tensions and impersonality of urban life; they are frustrated with streets paved with unemployment rather than gold. Indeed, following Clinard and Abbott's (1973: v) argument that "one measure of the effective development of a country probably is its rising crime rate," Shelley concludes that "the crime rate and the relationship between property and violent crime provide indices of a society's transition toward modernization" (1981a: 37). The second part of her thesis documents the major points of her first by case studies of England, France, Germany, Sweden, and pre-1917 Russia. Shelley compares these five countries, viewed in their premodern states, with present-day underdeveloped parts of the world. Their future is allegedly our past. Finally, Shelley repeats this pattern, predictably, in her analysis of socialist countries. Here, as she has done elsewhere,[3] Shelley tries to show that in some respects there are important "causal" differences between crime in capitalist countries and crime in socialist countries. But once again she sees the most important causal factor as modernization, overriding any specific cultural, economic, or political variation.

The advantage of Shelley's thesis about the causal influence of modernization is the great scope of its generality. It has, quite simply, almost universal application. This generality is also its greatest limitation. The method of agreement arrives at such impressive generalizations precisely because it altogether avoids complexity. However, simplicity and simplification must be distinguished. Shelley's basic explanatory tool is the concept of modernization; never is this conceptual deus ex machina discussed or identified. The social world of *Crime and Modernization* is one in which different countries are glibly labeled as developing, developed, capitalist, or socialist, no rationale is ever given for these assignations. The very concept of crime fares no better; crime is always and only seen as behavior proscribed by national legal authorities. Who are the criminals in this legalistic social world? Answer: roaming vagrants, members of the lower class, highwaymen, vagabonds, servants, primitive rebels, highly organized criminal groups such as those immortalized in Dickens' *Oliver Twist*. Where are the crimes of the rich and the powerful? Where are the crimes of one culture against another? Neither are at all recognized on this view.

At a few points in her thesis, Shelley begins to grasp the difficulty that cultural variation poses for the method of agreement. During a discussion of political crime, for example, she concludes that "these offenses are too subjective for comparison because the political system of each country determines whether such a category exists" (1981a: xiv). But why are "subjective" factors (whatever these may be) denied importance; why are "subjective" factors seen as pertinent only to certain kinds of crime; and how is the criminologist excluded from their sphere of influence? What value has comparative criminology if it dismisses subjective and cultural variation a priori? Such variation, if it exists, must be an integral part of cross-cultural research. For not altogether acceptable reasons, therefore, cultural variation represents an inconvenience to the elegance of the method of agreement, and is banished to the domain of the method of difference.

The Method of Difference

I have suggested that the method of agreement seeks to explain as many empirical cases of crime as possible by subsuming them under the aegis of a master theory. However, not even a master theory can explain every case of social behavior. The method of difference arises, therefore, largely from the empirical cases inexplicable to the method of agreement. The inexplicable cases encountered in investigations of the method of agreement automatically become the domain of the method of difference. As it happens, so dominant is the method of agreement in comparative criminology that few inexplicable or deviant cases have been discovered as yet. The method of difference operates exclusively only in Clinard's *Cities with Little Crime,* in Herbert's *The Geography of Urban Crime,* and in Gurr et al.'s *The Politics of Crime and Conflict* as a juxtaposition between Calcutta and three Western cities. Each of these three studies has different emphases: Herbert is concerned with the conceptual development of the ecological school, Gurr et al. with the rich texture of historical detail, and Clinard with innovation in the methodological understanding of crime rates. Let us look at Clinard's study of Switzerland.

Clinard's investigation in *Cities with Little Crime* begins at the very point where steadfast claims about modernization and rising crime rates fail. Switzerland is highly affluent, urbanized, and industrialized, and its populace has one of the highest rates of firearm ownership in the world. Yet, as Clinard notes, Switzerland "represents an exception to the general rule that a high crime rate accompanies a high degree of affluence, industrialization, and urbanization" (1978: 1). With the use of conventional data, Clinard suggests that the Swiss crime rate either remained fairly constant or actually declined between 1960 and 1971. These data included reports of crimes given to the police and conviction statistics on crimes with other sources collected in 1973. These include parliamentary debates in Zurich, media crime reports, and the deductible or premium ratios of Swiss crime insurance policies. Clinard's findings about the low Swiss crime rates are contrary to the generalizations about modernization and crime. At several points in *Cities with Little Crime,* Clinard juxtaposes Switzerland with other advanced countries. He notes, for instance, that both Switzerland and Sweden share certain features. Both are democracies with roughly similar demographic characteristics, large foreign worker populations, and strong currencies. Both have avoided wars for a century and a half. Why, then, is the Swiss crime rate so much lower than the Swedish?

Clinard explains the different crime rates by reference to salient parts of the Swiss and Swedish social structures. In Sweden, for example, the urbanization process was more rapid and produced larger cities and slums. There are no slums in Switzerland. Both are democracies, but Sweden is a centralized democracy that has tended to inhibit citizen initiative and responsibility for social problems such as crime. Switzerland is a decentralized democracy that strongly relies on the responsibility and direct action of individual citizens. The extensive and programmatic social organization of Sweden results in youthful boredom, reduced social control of the family, and pronounced youth subcultures. Crime rates are highest among Swedish youth. Switzerland stresses social conformity in the family and in school; it has the smallest percentage of married working women in Europe, and only in 1971 did Swiss women gain the vote in national elections.

The limited historical and empirical evidence in *Cities with Little Crime* does not, however, deter Clinard from advancing causal generalizations about crime. In his conclusion, Clinard (1978: 153-158) asserts that crime is not caused by economic disadvantage or poverty. It matters little to Clinard's argument, or mine here, that nowhere in *Cities with Little Crime* are notions like poverty and disadvantage addressed in depth. Clinard concludes that crime is caused by such factors as the spatial ecology of cities and the degree of political centralization. The solution to high crime rates, he infers, lies in smaller urban populations, political decentralization and the involvement of youth in sports and recreation.[4] Small is beautiful.

The reader must now be aware that the explanatory strength of the method of difference is its narrow focus on the intricate workings of one or two cultures. It is often associated, for example, in comparative history with the use of ideal types. However, the narrow focus of the method of diffe.ence is rarely innocent. Its very focus derives from cases inexplicable to the method of agreement, and whatever explanatory power it contains is parasitic on the method of agreement. The distillation of causal generalizations from limited historical and demographic data, therefore, is likely to occur at the conclusion of all studies based on the method of difference.

Methodological Relativism

The third method of comparative criminology arises from respect for cultural diversity. For relativism, the major obstacle to the construction of cross-cultural generalizations is the impossibility of precise equivalence of action and meaning in different cultures. How can homicide, for example, be compared in different cultures if each culture denotes a different range of social behavior as homicidal? How, and to whom, can cross-cultural generalizations be meaningful if cultures vary both in their moral, medical, and psychological attitudes to death, and in the seriousness of punishment they attach to homicidal deaths? Clearly, there is little purpose in our observing that an action in another culture does or does not seem homicidal to that culture if that observation is made solely in our terms.

Methodological relativism is a strategy that appears to allow an observer to devise cross-cultural generalizations while at the same time maintaining respect for cultural diversity. It operates at two levels. The first level involves appropriate adjustments of the instruments and observational techniques of research. Here, methodological relativism requires the observer, as Dixon (1977: 76) puts it, "to maximise his understanding of alien cultures by honest-to-God field work, moral charity, intellectual humility and a determination of the taken-for-granted assumptions of both his own and others' cultural milieu." The second level involves removal of the disjunction between the meaning systems respectively inhabited by the alien observer and members of the cultures observed. This level is a conceptual intervention.

The most sophisticated example of the first of these two levels of operation is still the method suggested by Wolfgang (1967). Wolfgang identified as problematic the reliability of international crime statistics.

Data such as those produced by Interpol, or published in the *United Nations Yearbook,* wrongly conflate widespread cultural variation in the definition and meaning of crime. Wolfgang proposed several reforms to rectify this situation. First, the diverse bases of national police statistics should be standardized. Second, the legal definition of crime should be abolished. The legal components of homicide, robbery, rape, and so on would be replaced by information about the type and extent of physical injury incurred and/or the pecuniary value of property damaged or stolen. With these changes, Wolfgang believed that cultural diversity would be retained even though specific legal definitions of crime, contained in natural data, would therefore be eliminated. Finally, Wolfgang suggested the use of a psychophysical weighting scale. A weighted rate of crime for each participating country could be had by obtaining, for each country, the sum of the frequency of each measured crime, then multiplying by its weight and dividing by a constant unit of population. But would such a scale really permit generalizations about national crime rates, despite cultural variation in the definition and meaning of crime? I think not.

Consider another type of methodological adjustment. Suppose that American criminologists wish to test the applicability of the theories of differential association and differential opportunity to Swedish youth. Suppose also that these theories are tested by questionnaire responses in Sweden. Several factors affect the precise translation of English words into Swedish, including lexicography, syntax, and the presence of translators. Can the concepts denoted by American theories be translated properly into the language and forms of life of Sweden without distortion of meaning? This very problem confronted Friday (1974) in his analysis of Swedish youth. Friday's (1974: 27-28) procedure was, first, to devise the questionnaire in English and to have it translated by two translators, one a Swede permanently living in the United States, the other a Swede living in Stockholm; second, to resolve discrepancies between the two translations by a third translator; finally, to retranslate the questionnaire into English. Friday indicated that this procedure "showed great consistency between the translators" (1974: 28), but he was forced to conclude that "some theories originating in the United States have no comparable meaning in Sweden" (p. 28).[5]

Friday was prompted to this conclusion not because his translators were consistently mistaken but because a key scale item for measuring differential opportunity (the American notion of "area") had no Swedish counterpart. No adjustments to Friday's research could have avoided this difficulty. It was not, note, the lack of fit between the research instrument (the questionnaire) and the Swedish social structure that led Friday to this conclusion. Research instruments can never occupy a neutral position between observer and observed; they are conceptual products and always operate through and with concepts. Rather, it was the simple lack of fit between American concepts and Swedish youth's own perception of the causes of their delinquency that forced this conclusion. A similar difficulty confronts Wolfgang's proposal to eliminate legal definitions of crime and replace them with "neutral" indicators— that is, assessments of pecuniary and physical damage. These indicators recommend, in fact, the mere substitution of one conceptual bias for another. Wolfgang's requests would still be answered by what national legal authorities designate as antisocial or criminal behavior, albeit differently described. Conceptual neutrality is not achieved in this way, either.

In the end, cross-cultural analysis always involves conceptual rather than technical or strictly empirical difficulties. This realization has produced the second level of operation within the overall strategy of methodological relativism. It consists in the attempt to understand other cultures with concepts that are not overtly culture-bound, concepts that therefore appear to be transcultural. Two good examples of this approach are found in Robertson and Taylor's *Deviance, Crime and Socio-Legal Control* (1973) and Newman's *Comparative Deviance* (1976). Robertson and Taylor's little book focuses on the problem of meaning in cross-cultural research. Its argument is profound and has been sadly ignored by recent authors in comparative criminology. Robertson and Taylor suggest that comparativists should refrain from the "crime in different countries" syndrome and instead focus on the relationships between controllers and controlled, between those who sanction and those who deviate. They also suggest that comparative research should proceed along four dimensions that transcend the peculiarities of any given culture: the degree of perceived authoritativeness of a norm; the degree of homogeneity of social control; the degree to which an alternative (criminal or deviant) culture is available; and the degree to which authoritative definitions are accepted by deviants. A second study (Newman 1976) is an important step in the development of comparative criminology because its focus is the imputed generality of cross-cultural perceptions of deviance and crime. These perceptions, Newman (1976: 34-35) argues, comprise six hypothetical and supposedly transcultural elements: the level of intensity of reaction to a deviant act; the respondent's own normative beliefs about the act; the respondent's definition of the act; societal reaction to the act; general public opinion about the act; and the respondent's perceptions of the activities of official controlling agencies.

The comparative method of Robertson and Taylor and Newman has two distinct advantages over its competitors. First, its conceptual indicators are both clearly defined and specific, and also general enough to transcend the unique features of different cultures. This advantage it shares with the method of agreement. Second, its comparative findings are not as predetermined as those of other methods; it has no prior allegiance to agreement or to difference. The greatest virtue of this second level of methodological relativism is that it appears to be anti-dogmatic. Further, its "wait and see" approach appears able to explain both similarity and variation among different cultures.

Each of the three major methods has its costs. The method of agreement tries to identify similarities among as many possible empirical cases of crime. The less sensitive or the more ethnocentric the users of this method, the more cases of crime they can explain, but no study based on the method of agreement can afford to ask thorny questions about cultural variation in the definition of crime or about subjective perceptions of the seriousness of crime. To ask such questions necessarily involves the rejection (see Black, 1976: ix-x; Shelley, 1981a: xiv) of the importance of vast areas of social life, areas addressed by "anti-scientistic" strategies like *verstehen* and hermeneutics generally.

Note the awful irony of the method of difference that is used in response to empirical cases which are exceptions to theories that use the method of agreement. The method uses the very accounts of crime rejected by the method of agreement. To understand Switzerland or Japan, for example, involves "getting inside" the practices and forms of life of those countries. The irony is, however, that no matter how successful the studies are that use the method of difference, the resultant explanation of deviant cases not only does not aid the theories that use the method of agreement but actually is entirely irrelevant to them.

What, then, of the third method — methodological relativism — and its relation to the search for generalizations in comparative criminology? Methodological relativism is undoubtedly more sophisticated than either of the other two methods, but in its empirical forms, it cannot be a solution to the real difficulties of cross-cultural comparison. What the first, or empirical, level of methodological relativism seeks, as we have seen with Wolfgang's proposals, is the rearrangement of the phenomena of crime in different cultures for the purpose of comparison. What this actually does, even for commendable reasons, is to rearrange and probably dissolve criminology as a coherent discipline. Whether or not the conceptual rearrangements of the second level or relativism avoid this danger, I must leave open to question here.[6]

RULES OF CONSTRUCTION:
A SUGGESTION

To those criminologists who count among their intellectual ancestry Montesquieu's *L'Esprit des lois,* Durkheim's *The Rules of Sociological Method,* and Malinowski's *Crime and Custom in Savage Society,* the charge that comparative criminology has produced no adequate generalizations must seem extravagant. But is it? In what does this charge consist?

By an adequate generalization about criminal behavior across cultures I understand, as Rheinstein understood the method of comparative law, those theoretically explicit and systematic attempts to uncover regularities that are "laws in the sense in which the term is used in the 'sciences,' laws of the kind of Newton's laws of gravitation or Gresham's law in economics" (1952: 99). In this sense, to generalize is to identify a law-like regularity in social behavior. It is to assert that the same event constantly recurs under the same conditions. Note that "under the same conditions" entails that a generalization only applies to what occurs under *conceptually* identical conditions. Cross-cultural generalization, in other words, necessarily ignores and even forbids cultural variation. As Glueck once expressed this, comparative criminology is a project designed "to reveal aetiological universals operative as causal agents irrespective of cultural differences among the different countries" (1964: 304).

The law-like generalizations to which Rheinstein and Glueck aspire are of the type "if p, then q, because z," where p is an initial antecedent event, q is a necessary consequence of p, and z is an explanatory postulate that enjoins p and q in a relationship of cause and effect. In these stringent, Humean criteria of adequacy, p is both a necessary and sufficient condition of q and also an invariant antecedent of q; p can properly be said to cause q if, and only if, p always precedes q and if q always follows p in time. How realistic is comparative criminology in aspiring to generalizations with these criteria of adequacy?

Consider Clinard and Abbott's assertion that "for developed societies, such as the United States and the countries of Europe, the most important causal factors [of crime] have been shown, generally, to be increasing urbanization and the persistence of slum areas" (1973: 1; bracketed words are mine). In the Humean sense—also the sense of Rheinstein and Glueck—if urbanization is a cause of rising crime rates, then urbanization must always precede rising crime rates, and rising crime rates must always follow urbanization. The application of these criteria are not without empirical difficulty when applied to social behavior. Some countries have experienced falling crime rates after urbanization. In some (and perhaps all) countries, factors other than urbanization have contributed to rising crime rates—the level of police activity, demographic changes, changes in criminal law, and so on. Turk (1981: 153) has reported some research suggesting that in Africa the attempt to *limit* urbanization has caused "substantial disaffection" with the processes of criminal justice. Clinard and Abbott's qualifying term "generally" now becomes rather important. Can rising crime rates have an infinitude of possible causes? Can the different causes of rising crime rates have an infinitude of possible consequences? These two questions raise even more difficult problems if it is typically true both that "urbanization precedes rising crime rates" (if p, then q) and that this generalization depends on conditional clauses about, for example, the interruption of kinship networks and the decomposition of religious belief.

I do not pretend, by way of conclusion, to have remedies for these difficulties. Comparative criminology's failure to establish adequate generalizations stems less from particular methodological defects, I believe, than from the fact that social behavior itself is not easily susceptible to the Humean regularities sought by criminologists. Social behavior is not of the same epistemic order as the behavior of forces, such as celestial bodies, in a physical system. Only with considerable discomfort can social behavior be compressed into the artificial straitjacket of a generalization. In the case of cross-cultural analysis, the discomfort of a generalization is tantamount to cultural imperialism. This lesson we should have learned from Malinowski, but even if understood the lesson cannot be heeded; the professional authority of criminologists, and social scientists at large, depends on their ability to generalize. With such resistance in mind, let me suggest some rules for the construction of cross-cultural generalizations about crime:[7]

(1) Crime in different cultures can be compared only if the definition and meaning of criminal behavior in these cultures are the same.

(2) An event p (e.g., urbanization) is not the cause of rising crime rates if it occurs when rising crime rates do not occur.

(3) p is not the cause of rising crime rates if it does not occur when rising crime rates do occur.

(4) p is not necessarily the cause of rising crime rates if one or more other variables (A, or A, B. . . n) is present in the same circumstances as p.

(5) For the generalization "p causes rising crime rates" to be intelligible, it must be explained by a theory.

NOTES

1. These findings were reported by Miracle (1981). Miracle submitted four sources to content analysis: the *International Journal of Criminology and Penology* (1973-1977); the first three volumes of the *International Journal of Comparative and Applied Criminal Justice* (1977-1978); the *British Journal of Criminology* (1950-1970); and the *Social Science Citation Index* (1972-1979). From these sources Miracle recorded "all publications containing any of the appropriate descriptors (e.g., crime, criminal, criminology, delinquency, law enforcement, penal, police, prisons, victimology, also specific types of crime) in the title" (1981: 383-384). My belief is that findings such as these are impaled on the very ethnocentrism that Miracle so studiously wishes others to avoid. His categories for cross-cultural research are none other than the concepts of American criminology. With different categories (e.g., trouble case, feud, dispute, self-help), Miracle's findings would have been very different and also more helpful.

2. This section has profited considerably from my having read the excellent account of comparative historical methods in Skocpol and Somers (1980).

3. The reader should compare the dull insensitivity of Shelley's *Crime and Modernization* with her highly original and important research on crime in the U.S.S.R. (Shelley, 1980).

4. Clinard has been criticized by Herbert (1982) for confusing cause and effect in the understanding of Swiss crime rates, and for not subjecting his "small is beautiful" thesis to rigorous testing. Herbert throughout eschews either comparative generalizations or conclusions about crime. Spatial and ecological theories of crime he consistently asserts to be at a very early stage of research.

5. This rejection of the American theory abroad is not, however, unique. American theories of crime have also been formally found inapplicable in the East End of London (Downes, 1966), Argentina (DeFleur, 1969), India (reported for Calcutta in Robertson and Taylor, 1973: 38), Poland (Mosciskier, 1976), and generally in underdeveloped countries (Sumner, 1982b). The majority of rejections to date have come from American researchers themselves; it will be interesting to see how much the rejection rate increases once criminologists in other cultures assert themselves in print in English. For earlier reservations about the applicability of American theories of crime elsewhere in the world see Robertson and Taylor (1973: 71, n. 21).

6. These rules essentially relax the strict procedural requirements of Human causality. See further Zelditch (1971).

REFERENCES

BEIRNE, P. (1983) "Cultural relativism and comparative criminology." Contemporary Crises.
BENNETT, R. R. (1980) "Constructing cross-cultural theories in criminology." Criminology 18: 252-268.
BLACK, D. (1976) The Behavior of Law. New York: Academic Press.
CAVAN, R. S. and J. J. CAVAN (1968) Delinquency and Crime: Cross-Cultural Perspectives. Philadelphia: J. J. Lippincott.
CHANG, D. H. [ed.] (1976a) Criminology: A Cross-Cultural Perspective (2 vols.). Durham: Carolina Academic Press.
— — — (1976b) "The study of criminology—a cross-cultural approach," pp. 1-137 in D. H. Chang (ed.) Criminology: A Cross-Cultural Perspective (2 vols.). Durham: Carolina Academic Press.
CHRISTIE, N. (1970) "Comparative criminology." Canadian Journal of Corrections 12: 40-46.
CLINARD, M. B. and D. J. ABBOTT (1973) Crime in Developing Countries: A Comparative Perspective. New York: John Wiley.
CLINARD, M. (1978) Cities with Little Crime: The Case of Switzerland. Cambridge: Cambridge University Press.
COHEN, S. (1982) "Western crime control models in the Third World." Research in Law, Deviance and Social Control 4: 85-119.
COLE, G. F., S. J. FRANKOWSKI, and M. G. GERTZ [eds.] (1981) Major Criminal Justice Systems. Beverly Hills, CA: Sage.
DOWNES, D. (1966) The Delinquent Solution. London: Routledge & Kegan Paul.
DURKHEIM, E. (1938) The Rules of Sociological Method. Chicago: Chicago University Press.
EDGERTON, R. (1976) Deviance: A Cross-Cultural Perspective. Menlo Park, CA: Cummings.
ENCINOZA, A. R. and R. del OLMO (1981) "The view from Latin America against transnational criminology." Crime and Social Justice 15: 61-67.
FRIDAY, P. C. (1980) "International review of youth crime and delinquency," pp. 100-129 in G. R. Newman (ed.) Crime and Deviance: A Comparative Perspective. Beverly Hills, CA: Sage.
— — — (1974) "Research on youth crime in Sweden: same problems in methodology." Scandinavian Studies 4: 20-30.
— — — (1973) "Problems in comparative criminology: comments on the feasibility and implications of research." International Journal of Criminology and Penology 1: 151-160.
GLUECK, S. (1964) "Wanted: a comparative criminology," pp. 304-322 in S. and E. Glueck (eds.) Ventures in Criminology. Cambridge: Harvard University Press.
GURR, T. R., P. N. GRABOSKY, and R. C. HULA (1977) The Politics of Crime and Conflict. Beverly Hills, CA: Sage.
HERBERT, D. (1982) The Geography of Urban Crime. London: Longman.
JANEKSELA, G. M. (1977) "Typologies in comparative criminal justice research." International Journal of Comparative and Applied Criminal Justice 1: 103-110.
LOPEZ-REY, M. (1970) Crime: An Analytical Appraisal. New York: Praeger.

MacINTYRE, A. (1971) "Is a science of comparative politics possible?" pp. 260-279 in Against the Self-Images of the Age. London: Duckworth.

MANNHEIM, H. (1965) Comparative Criminology (2 vols.). London: Routledge & Kegan Paul.

MARSH, R. (1967) Comparative Sociology. New York: Harcourt Brace Jovanovich.

MOSCISKIER, A. (1976) "Delinquency in Poland and the processes of industrialisation and urbanisation." Polish Sociological Bulletin 1: 53-63.

NEWMAN, G. R. [ed.] (1980) Crime and Deviance: A Comparative Perspective. Beverly Hills, CA: Sage.

— — — (1977) "Problems of method in comparative criminology." International Journal of Comparative and Applied Criminal Justice 1: 251-274.

— — — (1976) Comparative Deviance. New York: Elsevier.

— — — (1975) "Toward a transnational classification of crime and deviance." Journal of Cross-Cultural Psychology 6: 297-315.

— — — and F. FERRACUTI (1980) "Introduction: the limits and possibilities of comparative criminology," pp. 7-16 in G. R. Newman (ed.) Crime and Deviance: A Comparative Perspective. Beverly Hills, CA: Sage.

PARSONS, T. (1964) "Evolutionary universals in society." American Sociological Review 29: 339-357.

RHEINSTEIN, M. (1952) "Teaching tools in comparative law." American Journal of Comparative Law 1: 95-114.

ROBERTSON, R. and L. TAYLOR (1973) Deviance, Crime and Socio-Legal Control: Comparative Perspectives. London: Martin Robertson.

SEBBA, L. (1979) "The comparative method in criminology," pp. 15-36 in S. G. Shoham (ed.) Israel Studies in Criminology, Vol. V. Ramat Gan: Turtledove.

SHELLEY, L. I. (1981a) Crime and Modernization: the Impact of Industrialization and Urbanization on Crime. Carbondale: Southern Illinois University Press.

— — — [ed.] (1981b) Readings in Comparative Criminology. Carbondale: Southern Illinois University Press.

— — — (1980) "The geography of Soviet criminality." American Sociological Review 45: 111-122.

SKOCPOL, T. and M. SOMERS (1980) "The uses of comparative history in macrosocial inquiry." Comparative Studies in Society and History 22: 174-197.

SUMNER, C. [ed.] (1982a) Crime, Justice and Underdevelopment. London: Heinemann.

— — — (1982b) "Crime, justice and underdevelopment: beyond modernization theory," pp. 1-39 in Crime, Justice and Underdevelopment. London: Heinemann.

SZABO, D. (1975) "Comparative criminology." Journal of Criminal Law and Criminology 66: 366-379.

TARDE, G. (1902) La Criminalité Comparée. Paris: Felix Alcan.

TURK, A. (1981) "The meaning of criminality in South Africa." International Journal of the Sociology of Law 9: 123-155.

VETERE, E. and G. R. NEWMAN (1977) "International crime statistics: an overview from a comparative perspective." Abstracts on Criminology and Penology 17: 251-267.

WILKINS, L. (1980) "World crime: to measure or not to measure?" pp. 17-41 in G. R. Newman (ed.) Crime and Deviance: A Comparative Perspective. Beverly Hills, CA: Sage.

WOLFGANG, M. (1967) "International criminal statistics: a proposal." Journal of Criminal Law, Criminology and Police Science 58: 65-69.

ZELDITCH, M. (1971) "Intelligible comparisons," pp. 267-306 in I. Vallier (ed.) Comparative Methods in Sociology. Berkeley: University of California Press.

Maria Loś

3

University of Ottawa

ECONOMIC CRIMES IN COMMUNIST COUNTRIES

Crimes against the communist economic order and economic relations
are among the most publicized, widespread, and persistent crimes in
all communist countries. This article concentrates on selected forms of
economic crimes that threaten the principles of central planning of production and distribution of goods. My discussion is limited to the Soviet
Union and Poland, but the phenomena in question can be found to
exist in all Eastern European countries. As well, both their nature and
the attempts to control them are similar in all countries whose economic
systems follow the main principles of the Soviet economy.

It must be noted that most of the economic crimes in communist
countries do not have exact counterparts in capitalist countries due to
critical differences in the organization of their economies as well as in
the nature and scope of their criminal laws. Types of economic crimes
included in the criminal codes of all Soviet Republics involve engaging
in forbidden trades; falsifying figures or otherwise distorting reports
on plan fulfillment; private entrepreneurial activity; intermediary commercial operations; issuance of poor quality, nonstandard, or incomplete
products; and illegal manufacture, sale, and storage of alcoholic
beverages (*Great Soviet Encyclopedia,* Vol. 2: 66, the Criminal Code
of the RSFSR, Chapter 6, reprinted in *Luryi,* 1978: 171-175, and *Encyclopedia of Soviet Law,* Vol. II: 238-239). Thus, economic activities
criminalized in the Soviet Union are, with the exception of moonshining,
either legal or simply nonexistent in capitalist countries. Since the Cen-

*AUTHOR'S NOTE: I would like to acknowledge the contribution of two graduate
students of the University of Ottawa, Jadwiga Holenderska and Rebecca Volk, who helped
me to collect material for this chapter.*

tral Plan, according to which the communist economy is regulated, has the status of law, all economic deviations from the plan are criminalized. This implies a massive legal intervention in the economy as well as a reliance on the criminal law as one of the fundamental means of stimulating efficiency and excellence of economic production. Indeed, the penal law appears to play the role of a major regulator of the economy. For while traditional, capitalist regulators such as profit orientation, market laws, and labor negotiations are void of any meaning under communism, no new dependable regulating mechanisms have been developed.

CRIMES AGAINST THE CENTRAL PLAN

The aspirations of early communists to nurture a new kind of morality and a genuine commitment to the nationalized economy faded long ago through confrontation with popular dissatisfaction and workers' estrangement from the communist economic order. Not surprisingly, the coercive nature of the overcentralized and overplanned economy, based on the totalitarian principles of complete subordination of individual activity to an all-embracing program, has not promoted sentiments of coresponsibility and cooperation. The sense and purpose of any economic activity must be lost when its importance is reduced to the dry figures and indicators of the omnipotent plan which, in turn, do not correspond with the real production processes and real social needs. All that is required is a symmetry between the officially expected figures and the officially reported ones. Thus, a new form of alienation has been created: the alienation of the worker whose labor and productive effort is "paperized," converted into an official reality of the fulfilled (or unfulfilled) plan independent of the real material outcome and the conditions under which it was achieved. Since each level of the economic administration is interested primarily in transmitting positive messages about satisfactory production results to the higher levels, the bureaucratic circulation of paper effectively replaces the circulation of real products. Human labor does not result in commodities that are subordinated to the capitalistic market laws. Rather, it is turned into abstract figures, seductive playthings used by the rulers to support their ideological claims and political careers while further oppressing workers and repressing their desire for authentic production. The Central Plan, essentially a political tool of the exercise of power over the working people, helps not only to control but also to impoverish them. It facilitates a purely political management of the economy by the Communist Party elite which is afraid to face the complex economic reality. It desperately clings to the ideologically manufactured, fictitious images of a machine-like society, a society that follows precisely and eagerly all formal instructions and demands.

Participants of the productive process live in a constant fear that the discrepancy between the imagined and the real will be uncovered and they will be held responsible for producing this false reality. The irony is that, faced with no other option and under the threat of criminal and political sanctions regardless of culpability, they do in fact contribute to its creation, constantly turning real-life outcomes into well-rounded figures. In this well-planned system, both the failure to fulfill the plan as well as the provision of false information about its fulfillment are treated as criminal offences, antistate activities, and signs of disloyalty to the party. It is only the preparation of an unrealistic plan that is incompatible with reality that is not subjected to any legal sanctions or any other form of social control. It is exempt from scrutiny and criticism, sanctified by its party origin and ideological significance.

Under Soviet criminal law, a deliberate distortion by an official of accounting data concerning the fulfillment of plans is treated as a crime. Liability for additions was set by a decree of the Presidium of Supreme Soviet of the U.S.S.R. dated May 24, 1961, which emphasized the nature of such offences as antistate acts harmful to the national economy. According to article 152-1 of Criminal Code of the RSFSR, false reporting is punishable by deprivation of freedom up to three years (see *Great Soviet Encyclopedia,* 1973, Vol. 20 or *Luryi,* 1978: 1066).

While there are no special provisions in the Polish Penal Code, it does contain some more general categories of crime that can be applied to the cases of false reporting. For example, article 246, section 1 states that a public functionary who, exceeding his authority or failing to perform a duty, acts to the detriment of a social or individual good shall be subject to the penalty of deprivation of liberty for a period from 6 months to 5 years. Section 2 increases the maximum penalty to 10 years for cases where the perpetrator performs the act with the purpose of obtaining a material or personal benefit (*The Penal Code of the Polish People's Republic,* 1973: 102). This article of the penal code, however, is very rarely used by Polish judges (Spotowski, 1981: 10).

Report padding is a very common activity in all Soviet-style economies. It involves misrepresenation of the quantity, quality, or the very nature of economic output. Such operations often generate substantial profits for the management (and occasionally for the workers as well) by making them eligible for special financial bonuses resulting from the fulfillment or overfulfillment of the plan. While it usually involves reporting of fictitious achievements, in some cases, false reporting may also aim at concealing an excess portion of actual production. In these cases, this fabrication is done in order to avoid increases in the following year's plans or to build up reserves of materials or end-products to be used in cases of any future difficulties in achieving the planned quota. Naturally, report padding is frequently committed to cover up or to facilitate large-scale theft of state property or illegal production and/or illegal sales of produced goods.

In Poland, the habit of report padding is as widespread as in the Soviet Union. Numerous controls initiated by the Free Union Solidarity during its short legal existence confirmed that practically all the economic reports were false (see for example Monko, 1981 — an article published in Poland in a censored weekly magazine). Various other inquiries undertaken by Polish journalists during the same period lead to similar conclusions:

> Many bosses falsified statistics on their production and costs. Many went even further, selling goods which were not yet produced and accounting for them in the reports on the fulfillment of the plan [Oseka, 1981: my translation from Polish].

In 1980 an official from the Supreme Chamber of Control revealed during a session of the Polish Parliament that

> for years, the Supreme Chamber of Control was informing the leaders of the State and the Party of the dangerous phenomenon of fabricating statistics in order to show economic results better than the actual ones [Posiedzenie Sejmu PRL, 1980: my translation from Polish].

Yet, given these occurrences, law enforcement and other agencies of control are remarkably passive and reluctant to intervene. Even in the Soviet Union, despite strict legal provisions and special guidelines issued by the party and central legal agencies, law enforcers are rather cautious about this type of crime. Very few cases are investigated and prosecuted. Sanctions rarely involve the deprivation of freedom, which is the statutory penalty, and offenders are often allowed to continue in their managerial jobs or move to other posts of a basically similar nature.

With respect to many architects and organizers of eyewash — notably local state and Party dignitaries, leaders of provincial elite groups — local procurators are utterly powerless. *It may hardly be expected from the Soviet judge that he would eagerly send to a labour colony a respected comrade who engaged in what comrades in his position are routinely engaging in every day* [Pomorski, 1978: 305; italics added].

Practically all important local officials have an interest in the plan-related eyewash. They all have some official responsibility for overseeing that the plans for a given region are fulfilled. They all want to be left alone by the superior levels of command in order to continue with whatever illegal or semi-legal schemes they are involved in. Any reporting of unsatisfactory results threatens to bring outside controllers or investigators into their community. The existence of a tight network of mutual favours, corruption, and exploitation of state resources depends on a prudent and stable social environment. Such networks perpetuate themselves due to relationships of interdependence and support as well as a collective eagerness to participate in covering up all improper operations. Moreover, their impunity is greatly enhanced by the fact that they usually include most prominent local representatives of the police, the judiciary, and other legal agencies.

Any real attempt at more vigorous law enforcement and effective prevention of criminal report padding would have multiple negative effects for the central authorities as well. First of all, it is a crime committed almost exclusively by people in positions of relative power (which are held normally by party members) or at least with their direct knowledge and endorsement. Moreover, it is a crime they practically cannot avoid. A truly comprehensive law enforcement would mean the actual criminalization of this very large group of people on whom the party has to rely for everyday exercise of power. This, in turn, would have at least two politically undesirable consequences. First, it would officially label this key group as unworthy; second, it could provoke a hostile reaction and a further deterioration of relations between the central planners and the lower level managers. The party leaders could hardly afford such a move. Besides, they seem reluctant to obtain true production figures, since this would force them to make an embarrassing choice between, on the one hand, disclosing the truth about the dismal state of economy to the national and international public and, on the other hand, instructing the central statistical offices to disregard completely all the received reports and to prepare their global statistics purely on the basis of detailed political directives. This is not to suggest that at present statistics are not "doctored" on the central level, but it seems that at least some effort is made to go through the bureaucratic motions of summing up all the partial reports. If the productive units suddenly started to provide accurate figures, this exercise would be even more spurious and redundant.

Whatever the reasons for the nonenforcement, it must be realized that the crime of falsification of economic information is a crime of local establishment aimed at the central planners (see Pomorski, 1978). It is thus an expression of objective conflicts of interests within the dominant communist group. As such, it does not have a counterpart in capitalist countries. Its general acceptance and political usefulness do not alter the fact that it has a profound negative impact on the functioning of the communist economy. It prevents any realistic planning and leads to an escalation of a dangerous fiction, which becomes an organizing principle of the whole economy. An article in a Polish magazine published in 1981 talks openly about a "suffocation of reality by the paper fiction." The author observes:

> A false report becomes a starting point for erroneous planning, forecasting and style of management. False planning and false information about the plans and about the reality make it impossible to manage the economy [Monko, 1981; my translation from Polish].

As a rule, therefore, central planning gradually leaves "the terrain of reality and creates a fictitious reality which becomes autonomous from the real production" (Besançon, 1981: 43; my translation from French). Planning of production consists essentially of the planning of future statistics and not of future outputs.

It would be false, however, to claim that the fictitious functioning of the economy is caused by the prevalence of report padding on the local level. Such crimes against the Central Plan may contribute to the perpetuation and escalation of falsehood, but they are themselves necessitated by the very organization of the centrally planned economy. Any genuine critique of these processes, therefore, has to start with an analysis of the consequences that result from the principle of central control of the economy by a monopolistic political party, and not with its criminal abuses. Moreover, it must be noted that even if this principle has been proven economically unviable, it cannot be abandoned. Abolition of the central planning of the economy would precariously weaken the party's central control over the society. Economic and political control mechanisms simply constitute two sides of the same process and are based on the same set of structural principles.

CRIMES AGAINST THE
CENTRALIZED DISTRIBUTION OF GOODS

As is generally known, the centrally planned distribution of goods in communist countries is not very effective. And since the supply of goods is almost always insufficient and of poor quality, informal access to the legal as well as illegal system of distribution becomes one of crucial importance. Private middlemen and speculators play an extremely important role in an elaborate world of illegal or semilegal redistribution of foodstuffs, consumer goods, building materials, and other scarce commodities (see Simes, 1975; Grossman, 1977; Katsenelinboigen, 1977, 1978; O'Hearn, 1980, for more detailed analysis of Soviet illegal markets). It can be argued that such enterprising individuals or organized gangs introduce to the communist economy the capitalist market laws of supply and demand. Yet, in countries where all economic activity is supposed to be under the control of the government:

> The type of individual initiative which is widely considered praiseworthy in a country such as the United States, can be criminal. In fact, increasing success in individual economic endeavors tends to bring increasingly severe penalties, culminating in the death penalty for persons who are exceptionally successful [Barry and Barner-Barry, 1982: 305].

The problem is, however, that citizens of these communist countries seem to understand better the logic of the capitalist economy with its rivalry, injustice, and pursuit of profits, than the communist logic of repression and strangulation of private initiative through the strict controls of the central command. Their economic instincts urge them to search tirelessly for ways to redistribute scarce resources in order to most adequately satisfy the existing demand and ensure their own personal profit.

The Criminal Code of the RSFSR includes several crimes of this type:

> Art. 153. Activity as a commercial middleman carried on by private persons as a form of business for the purpose of enrichment shall be punished by deprivation of freedom for a term not exceeding three years with confiscation of property.

Art. 154. Speculation, that is, the buying up and reselling of goods or any other articles for the purpose of making a profit, shall be punished by deprivation of freedom for a term not exceeding two years with or without confiscation of property, or by correctional tasks for a term not exceeding one year, or by a fine not exceeding 300 rubles.

Speculation as a form of business or on a large scale shall be punished by deprivation of freedom for a term of two to seven years with confiscation of property [Criminal Code of the RSFSR reprinted in *Luryi*, 1978: 173-174].

In addition, speculation in currency or securities on a large scale is punishable by deprivation of freedom for 5 to 15 years with confiscation of property, with or without additional exile for a term of 2 to 5 years, or by death with confiscation of property. According to the Polish Penal Code, anyone without a commercial license who accumulates goods with the purpose of reselling them at a profit (art. 222), or anyone employed in a unit of the socialized economy who sells his own or another person's goods without authorization to do so (art. 223, s. 1), is subject to the penalty of deprivation of liberty for up to 3 years. But if in the commission of the latter type of crime the perpetrator is gleaning a regular source of income, the penalty is increased to a term of 6 months to 8 years (art. 223, s. 3). Moreover, anyone employed in a unit of the socialized economy who disposes of goods with the purpose of reselling them at a profit is subject to the penalty of deprivation of liberty for 6 months to 5 years. But if the perpetrator made the commission of such offences a regular source of income or if he has committed the offence in relation to property of considerable value, the penalty is increased up to 10 years (art. 221, The Penal Code of the Polish People's Republic, 1973: 95-96).

Despite their harshness, these laws do not seem to have a strong deterrent effect on potential perpetrators. Speculation is present everywhere, from agriculture to medicine. A typical example of the illicit redistribution of medical materials that is not well publicized in the Western literature but is nevertheless very common in communist countries is quoted in one of the issues of *Pravda:*

In a number of medical institutions in Baku, Kirovabad, Agdam, Yevlakh and other cities and districts in the republic, cases have come to light of the hoarding of medicines and their resale at high prices and the misappropriation of food intended for persons undergoing in-patient treatment [Tairov, 1979: 10].

Much better known in the West are numerous examples of speculation in meat, a commodity highly valued but always in short supply in both the Soviet Union and Poland. A recent report in *Pravda* indicates that in 1981 several hundred meat pilferers were detained in the southern Ukraine alone. Their method of operation is as has been described thus:

> The "miracle" begins when the carcass is placed on the slaughter shop conveyor for cutting. In places where a soiled or ragged spot should be gently excised, the butchers cut off a kilogram or two of good meat. Brisket, tenderloin and other parts of the carcass often wind up as trimmings. As carcasses are being processed, unauthorized personnel slip into the shop under various pretexts. Few leave without trophies. The directors of many farms. . . have complained about how their livestock "lost weight" at receiving centers and slaughterhouses [Kucherenko, 1981: 21].

It is not only the methods of committing crime that are typical in the described cases. The recommendations for reform often resemble the one proposed by a *Pravda* journalist:

> The selection and placement of personnel must be improved, as must upbringing work. Can one possibly consider normal the situation at the Odessa Meat-Industry Production Association, where Communists account for only 1% of the 800 employees who handle valuable goods or money? [Kucherenko, 1981: 21].

Since almost all goods are scarce in the Soviet Union and Poland, practically every factory has its own long record of pilfering, dealing, and reselling. The Soviet press is full of examples.

> The fence around the Dyatkovo Crystal Factory is full of holes, some big enough for a man to walk through, and a well-trodden path lies at the bottom of a ditch running under the fence. . . . Dyatkovo's market presents a depressing sight. Individuals carrying baskets and bags fearlessly offer a wide assortment of crystal at reasonable prices. "Peddlers" stroll through apartment houses and office buildings hawking items at the wholesale prices. The hotel is always full of characters who are "making contacts" [Pyrkh, 1982: 16].

And the recommendations for improvements are again typical: improved control, better checks at the factory gate, stricter methods of record-keeping, and so forth. In yet another case, a group of enterprising individuals sold tens of thousands of flowers at the marketplaces of large cities. This time, however, the product came from their own, legitimately owned plots.

> A person can grow anything he likes on his private plot, of course, but some speculators go so far as to build their own greenhouses for commercial purposes [Bablumyan, 1982: 19].

Thus, the very idea of producing something for profit is itself criminal. As well, it engenders further crimes since, in the case of the flower sellers, a private individual is not legally allowed to buy the necessary tools and materials to build a greenhouse and must, therefore, steal them from the nationalized economy or obtain them in the black market. Some Soviet journalists' recommendations concerned with the prevention of this type of crime are a bit more perceptive than those in previously quoted cases. For example:

> The speculation in flowers would not have such deep roots if the organization whose job it is to supply the public with flowers provided any serious competition for the private entrepreneurs. I have in mind the republic Ministry of Agriculture's Flora Association which fails to meet its flower-growing plans from one year to the next and whose products are far inferior in quality to those found in the marketplace [Bablumyan, 1982: 19].

Western commentators as well as "samizdat" authors in communist countries naturally go further in their interpretations of the role of black markets in a Soviet-style economy. For example, in an article circulated originally as a samizdat publication in Moscow, its author claims:

> The black market is the very basis of the Soviet economy, the foundation on which the planned economy structure rests. The black market is the socialist mechanism of power and exploitation, the very essence of our socio-economic system. . . . The commodities which circulate in it support the existing political and social order [Timofeev, 1982: 5].

His analysis concentrates on small rural plots that are officially intended to provide food for peasant families and are not supposed to develop into private enterprises whose production would be destined for black market sales. However, in his publication, Timofeev demonstrates that without these small peasant farms "the socialist economy would not survive a day" (1982: 8). Due to a total failure of the communist, collectivized agricultural scheme, these small allotments, based on private initiative and the peasant family's desire to survive, have been forced to adopt serious economic tasks. Indeed, "the share of the peasants' private parcels, with their 2½ percent of tilled land, is much more than half" of total agricultural production (Timofeev, 1982: 7). Not only does it feed all rural inhabitants (40% of the total population of the Soviet Union), but a significant portion is distributed in towns and cities through a network of illegal and semilegal markets. While many Western observers praise the efficiency of these private farms, they rarely realize at what human cost these results are obtained. They rarely appreciate the extent of Soviet rural exploitation where all able-bodied male inhabitants are forced to work all day for totally unprofitable collective farms almost without payment. Consequently, three-fourths of the work done on the private parcels is done by women, and much of the remaining work is performed by children and the disabled (Timofeev, 1982: 12). In Timofeev's words:

> A peasant family is a microcapitalist enterprise where the head of the family is required to exploit the labor of his dependents, to obtain from the personal farm the maximum surplus value and so make up for the necessary product not received by them on the collective and state farms. This exploitation is carried on, as a rule, by completely barbaric methods, without any modern agricultural methods, without machines, without the application of modern achievements.... Spade, wheelbarrow, sack, basket—these are almost the only tools [1982: 13].

Naturally, all obvious ways of increasing rationality of effort on these allotments, such as the unification of several plots or the purchase of more advanced tools and fertilizers, are strictly prohibited. By allowing them, the productive superiority of this private agriculture would become too obvious and the visibility of its success would be ideologically impossible to accept. As a result, their productivity is kept strictly under control and the distribution of their products is banned from legal markets. This capitalist form of economy and distribution is allowed to exist in order to feed the population, but it is publicly denied any legitimacy. It is submitted to numerous prohibitions and regulations in order to fix its productivity at an ideologically acceptable level, thereby preventing peasants from becoming economically independent agents.

> This thick web of prohibitions prevents the market from developing to full strength, prevents production from becoming directly connected with

consumer demand. The black market remains under the control of the administrative authority, which dictates harsh conditions of constant exploitation of the peasant on the collective farm, the state farm and the private parcel [Timofeev, 1982: 10].

These mechanisms are well analyzed in Besançon's "anatomy" of communism. He discusses the ambivalent attitude of the Soviet authorities toward those ever-present forms of capitalist production and distribution coexisting with the planned communist economy. The essence of his "realism principle" is well summarized in the following excerpts:

> The economy remains socialist... when the decision to make a compromise and to introduce some principles contradictory to the spirit of socialism constitutes a necessary price for maintaining power and, consequently, the possibility of promoting socialism in the future, when the opportunity arises.
>
> The principle that capitalism should be destroyed... is, thus, paralleled by another principle which says that enough capitalism should be preserved so the [communist] power will not be threatened by its own material and political base [Besançon, 1982: 52, 49; my translation from French].

Periodical antispeculation campaigns are supposed to achieve the same goals as other anticrime campaigns in communist countries—namely, to blame the "persistent remnants of capitalism" for the failures of communist economic and social policies. Thus, the very devices that are secretly designed to keep this economy going can be publicly held responsible for its unsatisfactory performance.

In Poland, speculation is as prevalent as in the Soviet Union. At the beginning of the 1980s, it became the target for a new anticrime crusade, initiated by the government desperate in the face of the growing Solidarity movement. The media were full of descriptions and condemnations of rampant speculation and growth of illegal markets. Special antispeculation squads were created that were manned by policemen, soldiers, and volunteers. They concentrated mainly on the most visible but relatively small-scale operators, while the activities of more serious wholesale dealers continued unhampered. The squads regularly raided flea markets and other places where private vendors were likely to be found. Newspapers reported daily on their successful operations as well as difficulties they had to face. The following citation illustrates well this carefully balanced political mixture of optimism and pessimism:

> It is true that after just two weeks of intensified antispeculation campaign, the black market is now on the defensive... Yet, we are still a long way from the total elimination of this unacceptable social phenomenon [Olszewski, 1981; my translation from Polish].

In just the first 7 months of 1981 these antispeculation raids on Warsaw private markets resulted in 212 cases being prosecuted by special penal boards and 98 referred to criminal courts. In addition, 233 speculators were fined on the spot ("Kontrola rynku," 1981: 8). This well-publicized war on speculation was expected to convince the public that an economic recovery of the country tormented by food shortages and general economic collapse depended mainly on the successful suppression of speculation and the operation of black markets. Such a task, it was implied, could not be accomplished by a free union movement, but rather only by full mobilization of the repressive forces in the society. A new bill on the "struggle against speculation" was hastily prepared proposing that almost unlimited power be granted to the police and special penal boards whose decisions, in turn, could not be appealed to the courts or to the prosecutor's offices. In addition, the proposed penalties were to be significantly more severe than the existing ones. Many lawyers and other social groups protested against the harshness and lawlessness of the proposed measures. A resolution of the Association of Defence Lawyers sharply criticized the draft, concluding:

> Only a socio-economic reform which would respect market laws, genuine workers self-governments and trade unions, and would secure appropriate prices and agricultural policy, could eliminate speculation or at least push it away from the mainstream of social life [Gorski, 1982: 2; my translation from Polish].

Debates on the antispeculation bill were stopped abruptly by the imposition of a state of war in Poland in December 1981, at which time temporary emergency laws were introduced. Despite great political changes, speculation has continued to be portrayed as one of the major aspects of the Polish economic crisis of the 1980s. And the voices demanding a radical socioeconomic reform in lieu of individualized criminal repression have once more been suppressed.

CONCLUSIONS

Economic crimes are defined in communist countries as

[such] socially dangerous activities, which infringe directly on socialist property relations, rules of production, trade and distribution of material goods, and which are contrary to general societal economic interests [Pawelko, 1971: 16; my translation from Polish].

This definition is based on an obvious mystification. It assumes that there exists an actual coincidence between general societal interests and the interests of the communist rulers who derive political power from economic relationships based on centralized ownership. The extraordinary protection the criminal law lends to these relationships represents the real nature of the power structure of communist societies.

Citizens seem to be well aware of the difference in the degree of legal protection extended to state property and to personal property. A survey of a representative sample of the Polish population conducted in 1975 found that 52.2% of the respondents believed that courts punished perpetrators of offences against "social" property more severely, while only 2.7% thought that they treated offenders against private property more harshly (35.5% assumed that the courts do not differentiate between these two types of offenders; see Gaberle, 1978: 154). There are many indicators, however, that private property is granted much more moral respectability and legitimacy than "socialist" property.

As was mentioned earlier in this chapter, the criminal law is officially portrayed as the main instrument for the control of economic abuses. It represents the individualized treatment of a global, organizational problem. It is clearly based on the principle of selective operation whereby more powerful perpetrators are protected from direct intervention by the law enforcement agencies. It also diverts attention away from defects in the organization of the economy and from the disastrous consequences of its total subordination to the political power centers.

Campaigns against economic crimes, as all other Soviet-style anticrime campaigns, are designed to play a mainly ritualistic function aimed at mobilizing official agencies and public opinion in support of general goals fixed by the party and the central planning agencies (see Smith, 1979, for a discussion of anticrime campaigns in the Soviet Union). These campaigns have shown a recurring pattern and their frequency has increased in recent years to keep pace with the clearly accelerated speed of economic decline. They are also coordinated with political pressures created by the five-year planning cycle, a fact that has been well documented in Smith's study of procuratorial anticrime campaigns.

> The overall trend of procuratorial supervision since 1968 has been associated clearly with the planning period. In the first two years of the plan, procurators supervise a wide array of violations.... But as the pressures to fulfill production quotas rise in the fourth year, procurators institute campaigns against theft and other economic violations which might threaten production. During the final year of the plan, particular attention is given to padding and falsification of reporting records [Smith, 1979: 153].

During these waves of mobilization of anticrime efforts and sentiments, there are always some people selected and sacrificed to fuel the campaign. By including, from time to time, some relatively high officials among the sentenced, it is hoped that the publicity will build up public trust in the impartiality of the legal system as well as provide further support for the claim that economic difficulties can be tackled by a diligent application of the criminal law.

In addition to these purely repressive measures, some attention is also paid to the idea of the prevention of economic crimes. Numerous recommendations can be found both in scholarly articles and the daily press advocating improvements in the social upbringing of citizens, in technology, and in the organization of production. Some authors locate the causes of widespread violations of "socialist economic relations" in the unsatisfactory state of social consciousness. They appeal for more educational work and for mobilization of the public sensitivity to the problem of economic crime. To quote but a few examples from the Soviet press:

> Many trade collectives and the system as a whole have not created an atmosphere in which there is a principled attitude toward violations of the rules of Soviet trade and abuses of office ["In the Azerbaidzhan," 1979: 10].

> There was a time when we could have attributed omission in upbringing work to material shortages and lack of training. Today, in conditions of developed socialism, those problems have basically lost their relevance. It has become increasingly important for every person to understand that he is personally responsible for law and order and for his capacity and ability to display his civic qualities actively [Anashkin, 1982: 20].

> The fight against thieves will not succeed unless each of us, regardless of rank, actively protects the people's property at his or her place of work [Orlovsky and Pankov, 1982: 16].

> When a hooligan offends a passerby on the street, we don't hesitate to call the police. What prevents us, then, from reporting a crook who insults everyone around him by brazenly living beyond his means on money stolen from other people and the state? [Rubinov, 1981: 17].

The origins of condoning attitudes toward corruption and economic crimes are often linked to the specific historical experience of a given nation. Demoralizing conditions of tsarist Russia as well as occupied and divided Poland are often quoted as important determinants of contemporary moral habits and attitudes of these societies.

Many Soviet and Polish authors discuss some desired changes in technical and technological aspects of production as well. Such changes are supposed to make it more difficult to commit crime and to facilitate its detection. The proposed measures include better protection of goods and tools, better methods of storage and conservation, more accurate instruments with which quantity, weight, and quality of goods are measured, improved technology and higher automatization of production, improved methods of bookkeeping, and gradual computerization of recording and of the whole process of circulation of information.

Finally, economic and organizational changes are occasionally recommended by the more critically inclined writers. While some of them concentrate on changes in organization and management of individual enterprises, there are others who go even further to suggest more global policy alterations. They may, for example, demand some modifications in the personnel and remuneration policies. It is interesting to note that there are basically two diametrically opposed approaches to this issue. One stresses the importance of political qualifications of the employees (e.g., "In the Azerbaidzhan" 1979: 10); the other argues that political criteria for important appointments and promotions within the economy and foreign trade are detrimental to the effectiveness of production and should be replaced by criteria related to professional qualifications and competence (e.g., Podgórecki, 1973: 187-188, and numerous Solidarity publications).

In addition, it is also emphasized by some commentators that a binding policy should be implemented whereby persons convicted for economic crimes should not be allowed to occupy executive positions or ones connected with considerable responsibility for state property or funds. One of the authors quotes astonishing findings of several Polish studies conducted in the 1960s proving that past convictions did not interfere with the future executive careers of many economic offenders (Pawelko, 1971: 181-182).

More general claims point to the persistent problem of inadequate supply and distribution of consumer goods, which not only stimulates but even necessitates the development of illegal production and marketing. It also increases the opportunities for illegal involvement by legitimate private producers. A comment in the Polish Communist Party's daily provides an example of such a concern.

> Harsh, determined and persistent actions [by the law enforcement agencies] bring some results, but without additional mechanisms it will not be possible to eliminate speculation completely. Naturally, the best solution would be an adequate supply of goods in the market, but this would not be of course possible in the near future [Olszewski, 1981; my translation from Polish].

In the words of a more academically inclined author:

> The preponderance of the demand over supply, which creates the so-called producer's market, is a criminogenic factor which contributes to various activities directed against state property and individual interests of the consumers [Pawelko, 1971: 191; my translation from Polish].

All these factors seem to play an important role in provoking or facilitating economic crimes; they are not, however, the actual primary causes, but merely the symptoms of an underlying malaise of the very foundation on which the communist economy rests (for a more detailed discussion see Loś, 1980, 1982). Moreover, they do not include the crimes against people that are committed daily on an enormous scale by communist industries and that involve disastrous levels of poisonous pollution as well as a drastic lack of consideration for safety standards and the needs of workers and consumers (see, for example, Ogórek, 1982: 5; "Pollution grows" 1982; Weschler, 1982: 167). It is generally forbidden to discuss these types of economic crimes, to propose changes, or to call for their more active prosecution. Only the crimes directed against some abstract economic principles are of an utmost importance to the Communist Party but are perceived as irrational and oppressive by the people, are given official publicity, attention, and political visibility. It is evident that their well-publicized prosecution is expected to reinforce the binding force of these fundamental, ideological principles and not to improve the lives of the citizens of communist countries.

REFERENCES

ANASHKIN, G. (1982) "The citizen, society and the law: personally responsible." Pravda April 16, p. 3. (Condensed in The Current Digest of the Soviet Press, "Tbilisi borough official shot for bribe taking," October 15, 1980, 32 (37): 14.)

BABLUMYAN, S. (1982) "Face to face with the law: flowers of evil." Izvestia, March 11. (Condensed in The Current Digest of the Soviet Press, April 7, 1982, 34 (10): 19.)

BARRY, D. D. and C. BARNER-BARRY (1982) Contemporary Soviet Politics. Englewood Cliffs, NJ: Prentice-Hall.

BESANÇON, A. (1981) Anatomie d'un spectre. L'économie politique du socialisme réel. France: Calmann-Levy.

Encyclopedia of Soviet Law (1973) F.J.M. Feldbrugge, ed. Leiden: Sijthoff.

GABERLE, A. (1978) "Poglady na dzialalność organów wymiaru sprawiedliwości skierowana na zwalczanie przestepstw przeciwko mieniu oraz stosunek do naruszeń mienia [Opinions on criminal justice agencies' activities directed against property crimes]," pp. 153-207 in M. Borucka-Arctowa (ed.) Poglady Spoleczeństwa Polskiego na Stosowanie Prawa [Opinions of the Polish Society on the Application of Law]. Wroclaw: Ossolineum.

GORSKI, K. (1981) "Adwokaci o walce ze spekulacja (Lawyers on struggle against speculation)." Zycie Warszawy, September 22, No. 220 (11836): 2.

The Great Soviet Encyclopedia (1973) New York: Macmillan/London: Collier-Macmillan.

GROSSMAN, G. (1977) "The second economy of the U.S.S.R." Problems of Communism 26 (5): 25-40.

"In the Azerbaidzhan Communist Party Central Committee" (1979) Bakinsky Rabochy June 21, 1979, p. 2. (Excerpted in The Current Digest of the Soviet Press August 29, 1979, 31 (31): 10-11 ["Azerbaidzhan: the shake-ups continue"].)

KATSENELINBOIGEN, A. (1978) Studies in Soviet Economic Planning. White Plains, NY: M. E. Sharpe.

——— (1977) "Coloured markets in the Soviet Union." Soviet Studies 29: 62-85.

"Kontrola rynku" [Market Control] (1981) Zycie Warszawy August 12 No. 186 (11802): 3.

KUCHERENKO, A. (1981) "With satirical pen: miracle conveyor." Pravda December 15, p. 6. (Condensed in The current Digest of the Soviet Press, January 13, 1982, 33 (50): 20-21 ["State and law"].)

LOŚ, M. (1982) "Crime and the economy in the communist countries," pp. 121-137 in P. Wickman and T. Dailey (eds.) White-Collar and Economic Crime. Lexington, MA: D. C. Heath.

——— (1980) "Economic crimes from a comparative perspective," pp. 251-293 in G. R. Newman (ed.) Crime and Deviance: A Comparative Perspective. Beverly Hills, CA: Sage.

LURYI, Y. [ed.] (1978) Soviet Law and Legal System. Toronto: York University, Osgoode Hall Law School.

MONKO, M. (1981) "Blad" [Mistake]." Solidarnosc, April 10, 2: 2-3.

O'HEARN, D. (1980) "The consumer second economy: size and effects." Soviet Studies 32 (1): 218-234.

OGOREK, M. (1982) "Szczelny szlam" [Tight slime]." Polityka May 29: 5 26 (15).
OLSZEWSKI, J. (1981) "Akcje kontrolne nie ustaja. Spekulacja nie moze sie oplacac [Control operations continue. Speculation cannot pay]." Trybuna Ludu August 15-16.
ORLOVSKY, G. and M. PANKOV (1981) "Returning to what was printed: the end of underground firm." Sovetskaya Rossia December 13, p. 6. (Condensed in The Current Digest of the Soviet Press March 24, 1982, 34 (8): 15-16 ["Bribers land behind bars, join officials they 'bought' "].)
OSEKA, J. (1981) "Z czym na dywanik [What should be scrutinized]." Polityka November 18, 25 (8/1251): 6.
PAWELKO, W. (1971) Zapobieganie Przestepstwom Gospodarczym [Economic Crime Prevention]. Warsaw: PWN.
The Penal Code of the Polish People's Republic (1973) The American Series of Foreign Penal Codes. South Hackensack, NJ: Fred B. Rothman/London: Sweet & Maxwell.
PODGÓRECKI, A. (1973) Diagnostyczny Obraz Niektórych Trudnych Problemów Spoleczeństwa Polskiego oraz Refleksje Socjotechniczne [Diagnostic Picture of Some Difficult Problems of Polish Society and Sociotechnical Recommendations]. Warsaw: University of Warsaw.
"Pollution Grows in Eastern Europe" (1982) New York Times, September 12.
POMORSKI, S. (1978) "Crimes against the central planner: "Ochkovtiratel'stwo,' " pp. 291-317 in D. D. Barry, G. Ginsburgs, and P. B. Maggs (eds.) Soviet Law After Stalin, Part II: Social Engineering Through Law. Alpen aan den Rijn: Sijthoff & Noordhoff.
"Posiedzenie Sejmu PRL [A Meeting of the Polish Parliament]" (1980) Zycie Warszawy November 22-23, 275: 4.
PYRKH, I. (1982) "The ring of crystal was heard from afar. The Dyatkovo plant takes a carefree attitude towards the theft of valuable articles." Sovetskaya Rossia March 14, p. 6. (Condensed in The Current Digest of the Soviet Press, April 21, 1982, 34 (12): 16 ["Million-ruble pilferage feeds brisk market in crystalware"].)
RUBINOV, A. (1981) "Diamond hands. About people who live beyond their means." Literaturnaya Gazeta July 1, p. 13. (Condensed in The Current Digest of the Soviet Press November 4, 1981, 33 (40): 17 ["How to curb the high-living 'Underground' millionaire?"].)
SHENFIELD, S. (1982) "Pripiski: false statistical reporting in Soviettype economies." Presented to the Conference on Corruption, Birmingham, June (Organized by Centre for Russian & East European Studies).
SIMES, D. K. (1975) "The Soviet parallel market." Survey 21 (3): 45-52.
SMITH, G. B. (1979) "Procuratorial campaigns against crime," pp. 143-167 in D. B. Barry, F.J.M. Feldbrugge, G. Ginsburgs, and P. B. Maggs (eds.) Soviet Law After Stalin. Part III. Alpen aan den Rijn: Sijthoff and Noordhoff.
SPOTOWSKI, A. (1981) "Przestepstwa naduzycia sluzbowego." Solidarność, May 29, 9: 10.
TAIROV, L. (1979) "Unity of word and deed." Pravda July 19, p. 2. (Condensed in The Current Digest of the Soviet Press August 29, 1979, 31 (31): 9 ["Azerbaindzhan: the shake-ups continue"].)
TIMOFEEV, L. (1982) "Black market technology in the U.S.S.R.: or the peasants' art of starving." Telos 51: 5-21.
WESCHLER, L. (1982) Solidarity: Poland in the Season of Its Passion. New York: Simon & Schuster.

Elmer H. Johnson
Southern Illinois University

4

MEDIATION IN THE
PEOPLE'S REPUBLIC OF CHINA
Participation and Social Control

Mediation has been described as the most striking feature of the legal system of the People's Republic of China (PRC), with adjudication regarded as a last resort because, unlike mediation, it terminates controversies without the consent of the disputants (Cohen, 1966: 1201). I was a member of a group of American criminologists, lawyers, and criminal justice specialists who were the guests of the Ministry of Justice in experiencing various facets of criminological phenomena in the PRC.[1] Among those experiences was exposure to the process of mediation there. This chapter records my exploration of the implications of the mediation work observed there.

DISTINCTIVE ELEMENTS OF MEDIATION

Adjudication and mediation are usually presented as polar opposites. Felstiner (1974: 69-75) outlined the distinguishing elements for these two forms of dispute settlement. In adjudication by a formal legal system, the third party is acknowledged to have the power to specify the outcome of the dispute; the behavior of the disputants is evaluated against generalized rules of behavior; the focus of attention is on the "facts" rather than on normative shifts by the disputants; and the losing party is likely to be more impressed by the coercive power of the court than of his original error. The expertise of adjudication is in knowledge of the rules for judgments and of the rules for evaluating the conduct of disputants. Then it is possible to mass-produce decision makers for the process of adjudication, as in law schools.

In mediation, the third party must obtain the consent of the disputants to the proposed solution without coercion; the mediator constructs the outcome out of the sociocultural context of the dispute rather than relying primarily on preestablished rules; the focus of attention is on the framing of a solution acceptable to the disputants as they idiosyncratically view the controversy; and the disputants are likely to view the outcome of successful mediation as generally acceptable without the bitterness engendered by coerced compliance. "Mediation flourishes where mediators share the social and cultural experiences of the disputants they serve," Felstiner (1974: 74) says, "and where they bring to the processing of disputes an intimate and detailed knowledge of the perspectives of the disputants." These characteristics of mediation, he says, usually obstruct the mass production of mediators.

The distinctions encourage one to believe that mediation holds potential for correcting some of the criminal justice problems that go with adjudication. The span of criminal justice responsibilities may be narrowed by this alternative mode of dispute settlement particularly for minor offenses, and the excessive caseloads of criminal justice agencies are reduced for the sake of more effective coping with serious crimes. This form of dispute management promises to release the forces of informal controls within the context of "natural" communal forces to maintain social stability and minimize deviance through convergence of the social interests and self-conceived private interests of individual members of society. The alienative effects of coerced adjudication may be circumvented by the necessity that the mediation process receive the consent of the disputants and that conflict be resolved in terms that make sense to them within the context of their living environment. Fulfillment of these necessities is promoted when the mediator is identified as a regular participant in that environment, rather than a representative of a control bureaucracy imposing a decision according to preestablished rules that serve interests other than those of the disputants and of the immediate group of which they are members.

PUBLIC PARTICIPATION AND MAOIST IDEOLOGY

The features of mediation work in the PRC must be assessed within the context of the dedication of Maoist ideology to mobilizing the "masses" in support of the creation of a socialist society. Townsend (1967: 47, 72-76) provides the ingredients for a summary statement.

As a consequence of the problems of the Chinese Communist Party in gaining an organizational foothold prior to 1935, Mao Tse-tung became convinced in the invincibility of mass movements and their potential as revolutionary weapons. The "mass line" instructs party members to maintain constant contact with the workers and peasants, listening to them, experiencing their living, and working with them. Otherwise, "bi eaucratism" would prevent the party's representation of the people and its successful leadership of the revolution.

The policies are framed by learning from the masses, but the party makes the actual decision on what is "correct" because of its superior knowledge and experience. The policy is taken to the masses for execution, but not through enforced obedience. All available media are to inform the masses, raise their level of understanding and political consciousness, and thereby obtain conscious popular implementation of the policy. Extensive participation in the political process entails execution rather than formulation and control of policy. The mass line blurs the distinction between government and nongovernmental activities; public acceptance of policy is sought through use of state organs, propaganda media, mass organization, and direct contacts between functionaries and the masses.

Contradictions can exist among the people and between the government and the masses because the socialist system is not fully consolidated. The contradictions exist not because of conflicts between socialism and the people's true interest, but because organs still suffer from bureaucratism and other flaws, some of the masses have not learned the system, government workers need experience, and so on. Contradictions are to be solved by distinguishing right from wrong as determined by what is beneficial to the socialist transformation and a strong Communist Party. Those demands that do not meet this standard are to be heard but only so they can be corrected. When a member becomes alienated from the group, he is to be subjected to criticism by others and also to engage in self-criticism for the purpose of correction that reintegrates him into the group (Dittmer, 1974: 336-337).

Political activity must be conscious, and political consciousness is attained with understanding the political significance of one's behavior and some degree of acceptance of communist ideology. By raising the popular level of ideology, the construction of socialist society will be promoted and the communist achievements will be made permanent. In light of the thousands of years of feudalism before Socialist Liberation, constant and penetrating education must be undertaken to deal with antisocialist ideas. All citizens are urged to observe labor discipline (coming to work on time, and meeting production quotas), preserve public order, guard state secrets, watch suspicious persons, and help suppress all acts endangering public security.

COMMITTEE MEMBERS DESCRIBE THEIR WORK

Our conference on mediation committees was conducted in the administrative office of the Shin Zhu Gang subregion of Nanking. Over 40,000 persons reside in the subregion representing some 10,000 households. Within the subregion there are 11 mediation committees. In the first 10 months of 1982, the committees had mediated 103 civil cases: 47 neighborhood disputes, 19 family disputes, 9 marriage disputes, 19 housing disputes, 6 traffic cases, and 3 other cases. Since the mediation committees do not handle traffic incidents, the six traffic cases were minor incidents, such as a quarrel stemming from a person pushing a bicycle hitting another person. The membership of the committees was described as follows:

> All of the members are elected on a democratic basis. One member is elected as director and another as deputy director of the committee. Members usually are retired government functionaries or retired workers. They receive no salary. The requirements for membership are in ideology, in work style, in personality, and in having the respect of people. There is some kind of training once they are elected. Usually once a month study will be organized in the policies, laws and decrees of the government. At times also the legal workers of the People's Courts will help them to learn and understand laws. Usually, the term is for two years. All members can be reelected. If a member fails to receive enough support from neighbors, he can be dismissed any time during the term. When the member gets work elsewhere or moves his residence from the area, he is also dismissed.

The mediation process was described largely by presenting several cases, rather than providing an analytic interpretation of the fundamental principles. (This descriptive approach is to be expected among those intimately involved in intimate relationships with clients and charged with the responsibility of applying highly generalized principles of a far-flung program.) One of these cases serves our need for illustration.

There was an older lady named Liu and a young man, Chung. In July or August 1981, the young man wrote an article published in a Nanking newspaper concerning the parents' interference in the marriage of their children. The older lady became angry because she thought the article referred to her. Wherever she saw the young man, she would call him names. When made aware of the case, the mediators went at once to her home and told her that the article chiefly concerned an abnormal phenomenon in the society, not directly related to her family affairs. "It is no good that you scold him. Your two families used to be on good terms. Your scolding is not conducive to the emotional harmony of the place." After repeated persuasion, the older lady was not convinced.

One day, two boys of the two families, playing with toy guns, had a quarrel; as a result, the wife of Chung bit the finger of the Liu boy. The mediator hurried to the spot and stopped the fighting. The leading members of the working union, where the two families were working, called a meeting in which both families were required to carry out self-criticism. The old lady was told she was wrong in calling the author shameful names. It was said that he had done well in writing the article, but he was required to adopt an appropriate attitude and method of reasoning. The old lady was required to pay two huan to treat the bite. But the mediation failed to end the disharmony between the two families.

Then we had the matter of the Fourth Duty.[2] With the help of this duty, the mediators worked persuasively with the old lady. She was told that if the two families continued quarreling, it was not good for the whole society, as well as adversely affecting the other families in the neighborhood. It was not helpful to the maintenance of the good social order. As a result of the mediation work, her political consciousness was raised to new heights. At that time there was a quarrel between the husband and wife of the Char family. The old lady went to the Char family and played an active role in settling the dispute. This action pleased the Chung family. Now the two families live on even better terms than before the quarrels.

The spokesperson for the mediation committees summarized their purposes:

> By way of mediation we propagate the policies and laws of the state and reduce the contradictions and disputes among the people. As a result, the committees can reduce by a very great number the cases that would be submitted to the People's Court for settlement. At present the main task facing all of China is to develop the economic base, calling for an even greater level of performance in mediation for the sake of a stable order and the unity of the country. We should do our work well to develop the formation of the country.

> The first aspect of our mediation work is to raise the political consciousness of the people so as to prevent civil disputes. Second is to mobilize the masses of the people. Third is that, once a potential dispute is discovered, it is settled at the very beginning—to nip it in the bud, to reduce the intensity of the dispute.

DECENTRALIZED DECISION MAKING?

At first glance the mediation committees appear to be examples of grass-roots decision-making specified variously in calls for participatory democracy. Cook and Morgan (1971: 4) note two features common to differing proposals: First, authoritative decision making would be decentralized or dispersed downward from the top of administrative hierarchies to bring authority closer to the people affected by it. Second, persons involved directly in decision making would include those without credentials as formally trained experts or as career professionals.

Decentralized decision making is one of the means of reducing the inertia of criminal justice bureaucracies and of cultivating responsiveness of criminal justice processing to the informal controls of the local communities. American proposals for decriminalization, deinstitutionalization, and diversion convey such arguments. Identifying bourgeois criminal justice as exploitive, radical criminologists advocate a popular justice model that would emphasize resolution of disputes by people themselves in their own communities and workplaces in their own terms (Quinney, 1977: 291). Whether the change agenda is that of liberals or radicals, the greater involvement of amateurs in criminal justice affairs has been advocated.

Mediation in the PRC does not qualify as an example of the decentralization of authoritative decision making. Public participation in dispute settlement is strongly encouraged but in execution rather than in the formulation and control of policy. As said in Nanking, mediation is a means of propagating the policies and laws of the state, of maintaining a stable order, and of strengthening the unity of the PRC. The ultimate purpose is "to mobilize the masses of the people" by raising the political consciousness of those persons in dispute.

The communist ideology, Lubman (1967: 1357) notes, regards conflict as "the very stuff of social and political process. Individual disputes, while regrettable, are regrettable not so much because they impair the relationships between the disputants as because they interfere with important national tasks. The party objective in handling these interferences is not merely to repair damaged relationships or even to improve production, but to use the dispute by resolving the contradictions it represents, correcting the disputants' ideology and standpoint, and reaching a result consistent with national policies.

MEDIATION:
THE WORK OF AMATEURS

Ordinary people are directly involved in the mediation work in opposition to the principle that specialized training and professional status are crucial to criminal adjudication. The mediation process operates within a population congestion that makes almost inevitable intimate knowledge of one's neighbors' conduct and affairs. The ingredients for lay participation in mediation also are present in the centuries-old preference for mediation through Confucian regarding of the adjudication as a regrettable necessity, a traditional emphasis on the precise setting in which a dispute occurred, avoidance of the expense of going to a traditional court, and the greed, corruption, and insolence of the functionaries of those courts. Then, quarrels were highly likely to be settled within the family, the clan, the village, or the trade guilds (Cohen, 1966: 1206, 1212-1222). Although communists have fundamentally revised the traditional mediation style by demanding political activism, the willingness of persons to undertake mediation, their preference of it over adjudication, and their acceptance of a third party echo centuries of Chinese history.

Election of the mediators by neighbors possibly legitimates their work in the eyes of the disputants. The official criteria for their eligibility include "personality and having the respect of the people." Members failing "to receive enough support from neighbors" may be dismissed. These criteria suggest official recognition and general awareness of the importance of those interpersonal skills that enable the mediator to win the consent of the disputants to be involved in mediation. Those skills are applied effectively when the mediator knows well the sociocultural parameters of the situation within which a compromise can be worked out.

The ideal mediator is described as one who hurries to the scene when the dispute is reported. In Nanking there was emphasis on the importance of "nipping the dispute in the bud" to reduce the intensity of the dispute. Mediation is more likely to be successful if the dimensions of the dispute are kept narrow, if the disputants do not have time to fuel their passion, and if other persons do not become involved. Rapid dispute resolution minimizes disturbance of neighborhood harmony but also reduces the opportunity to use the situation for ideological instruction of the disputants and the populace in general. Rapid mediation depends on the involvement of the mediator in the local community to be able to receive an early report of the incident and his ability to assess the disputants and the dispute quickly for rapid management of the incident.

Mediation in the People's Republic cannot be described as pure grassroots participation because of politicization and the limitation of the public participation to the execution of the policy to be supported through mediation. Nevertheless, the work of mediation cannot be discounted as merely that of systematic propagandizing, "Model mediators cannot be dismissed as stage people, however superficial their reported words and deeds may seem to foreign readers skeptical of propaganda," Lubman (1967: 1323) says. Although they represent ideals, they also represent the expectations and desires that have often been substantially realized by a leadership that, at least in the past, has known well the people it leads. The "mass line" serves political purposes, but it also calls for cadres to be in constant and intimate contact with the lives of workers and peasants. The admission that contradictions exist and the party's constant emphasis on raising the popular level of ideology lend credence to the view that mediation is often more dispute-oriented than propagandistic, even when the mediators are activists.

In conclusion, because by definition it must obtain the consent of disputants and avoids forced solutions by meeting their idiosyncratic interests, mediation must be examined as a process carried out within a particular sociocultural milieu. We have examined briefly the Maoist ideology to obtain clues to the rationale and purposes of mediation in the People's Republic of China. The descriptions of those persons engaged in mediation work in Nanking have been used as a framework for considering some selected features of that work as expressions of the social system of the PRC. From the perspective of comparative criminology, it is appropriate that our examination be carried out in this fashion. Also from this perspective, comparative studies enable us to take a fresh look at familiar concepts as they are applied in our own social system. Arbitrary comparisons violate the caution that each system must be studied in its own terms, but mediation in America may be explored more fruitfully as we learn more about its special meaning in a fundamentally different system.

NOTES

1. The visit in November-December 1981 was part of the People-to-People Program, Spokane, which has sponsored delegations of citizen leaders and professionals since 1956 to accept invitations of foreign countries to observe particular activities. In this project the Ministry of Justice arranged meetings with the government leaders, judges, law enforcement and correctional officials, legal educators, research groups, and the like in travel that began in Beijing and ended in Shanghai.

2. The four duties are duty on behavior, on language, on soul, and on environment or circumstances. The latter duty entails preservation of social harmony.

REFERENCES

COHEN, J. A. (1966) "Chinese mediation on the eve of modernization." California Law Review 54: 1201-1226.

COOK, T. E. and P. M. MORGAN [eds.] (1971) Participatory Democracy. New York: Harper & Row.

DITTMER, L. (1974) Liu Shao-ch'i and the Chinese Cultural Revolution. Berkeley: University of California Press.

FELSTINER, W.L.F. (1974) "Influence of social organization on dispute processing." Law and Society Review 9: 63-94.

LUBMAN, S. (1967) "Mao and mediation: politics and dispute resolution in Communist China." California Law Review 55: 1284-1359.

TOWNSEND, J. R. (1967) Political Participation in Communist China. Berkeley: University of California Press.

QUINNEY, R. (1977) Class, State and Crime: On the Theory and Practice of Criminal Justice. New York: David McKay.

Philip Jenkins
Fred Hutchings
Pennsylvania State University

5

NEW PATTERNS OF URBAN RIOTS
Miami and Liverpool

When examining British social problems in the late 1960s, politicians and scholars often expressed the hope that the nation would never achieve American levels of civil violence. With the race riots of that decade much in mind, the United States became for Britons a horrible warning. In 1970, for example, an article about West Indians in Britain asked 'Must Harlem come to Birmingham?' (Hall et al., 1978: 21-28). In light of recent events, such comparisons naturally appear unfair and rather ironic. With the exception of the events in Miami in 1980, the United States has been free for some 12 years of major urban riots; while disorders in Britain have become increasingly frequent, and culminated in the massive street riots of July 1981.

It therefore appears, as if in terms of civil violence, Britain in the 1980s has developed close resemblances to the United States in the last two decades. There are apparently close parallels between, say, the events in Miami in 1980 and those in Toxteth (Liverpool) in 1981. If this is indeed the case, then such parallels are important. Findings about the causes and nature of riots in one country may help to illuminate events in the other, and this has serious implications for policymakers. For instance, in the immediate aftermath of the British riots of July 1981, copies of the Kerner Commission's report on American disturbances

AUTHORS' NOTE: We are grateful to Professors Edwin Donovan, Peter Meyer, and Stephen Mastrofski for their helpful comments on earlier drafts of this chapter. We would also like to thank Fergus Nichol of London's Bookmarx Club for his generous assistance in locating material.

in the 1960s were being avidly sought by British M.P.s and Cabinet ministers.

We wish to show that such parallels did indeed exist, and were perhaps even closer than has been suggested. In particular, racial resentments focused on the issue of high unemployment and a perceived threat from right-wing terrorism; while the justice system was seen as deeply biased against the poor and unwilling to punish even the most blatant breaches of discipline by police officers. But at the same time, the contrasts between British and American events are so profound as to throw into question the value of any analogies one government might be tempted to draw from the experiences of the other. For example, British events were characterized by little (if any) of the ethnic hostility and conflict between racial groups that were so marked a feature of the Miami events. They were much more politically motivated, rioters being inspired more by a sense of class rivalry. We will attempt to explain the reasons for these fundamental differences between the two movements: whether they arose from the dissimilar nature of the two societies, or whether they resulted from the idiosyncratic nature of political developments in Britain.

However, a central theme will be that both recent types of riot, the British class riot and the Miami race conflict, represent a new departure from the 1960s patterns described by Kerner. Both resulted from the economic and political crisis of the last decade, so much more fundamental than that of the 1960s; and each represents in its own way a disturbing portent for the future.

SIMILARITIES

When examining the rioting of 1980 and 1981, both the British and American media agreed on one basic point. The violence had been different in some respects from that described by the Kerner Commission in the 1960s, but the basic causes and explanations remained valid. Few analyses failed to cite Kerner, and most agreed with *The Nation* that the Commission "gave us about as comprehensive a set of answers as we are ever likely to get" (*Nation*, May 31, 1980: 644). In Britain, terms like "race riot" were studiously avoided, but Kerner parallels were drawn nonetheless. American sources suggested that Britain was now, at last, beginning to face the problems the United States had suffered 15 years before.

If we compare the three sets of events—American cities 1964-1968; Miami 1980, and Britain 1980-1981—we can find considerable evidence to confirm the view of essential similarity (Kushnick, 1981). Some of the resemblances need little explanation. For instance, all the riots tended to last for similar times. That is, it took a similar number of days for the police to organize an effective response and for the rioters to grow tired and to exhaust easy targets for looting. Equally, it is not surprising that riots tended to happen in waves. From one epicenter, violence spread to other cities with similar problems and grievances. In 1967, a riot in Tampa was followed in the same week by fighting in Cincinnati and Atlanta and by trouble in Newark and Detroit. The following month, the latter two cities produced some of the most serious civil violence of the decade. In Britain, a riot in Southall on July 3, 1981 had inspired even larger violence over the next four days in Brixton, Liverpool, and Manchester. By July 12 there had been violence in 20 more cities (Kettle and Hodges, 1982).

Of course, it is difficult to draw comparisons between the scale and nature of the violence in the two countries. For both police and rioters, firearms are infinitely easier to obtain in the United States than in Britain. This goes far in explaining the different number of casualties: one dead and a number maimed in *all* the British riots of 1980-1981, as compared to 34 killed in Watts in 1965, 43 in Detroit in 1967, and 18 in Miami in 1980. However, the lack of guns should not lead us to understate the scale of violence in Britain. In Liverpool, rioters' tactics against the police included spreading gasoline across streets and igniting it; dropping television sets from high building; and driving concrete mixers and other heavy vehicles at police lines. Thus, we suggest that the difference in casualty figures does not indicate any basic difference in the scale of British and American rioting.

Resemblances between events in both countries became very close when we compare the official reports produced after each eruption, and especially the list of causal factors cited. The Kerner Commission categorized grievances into three levels of intensity:

First Level

1. Police practices
2. Unemployment and underemployment
3. Inadequate housing

Second Level

4. Inadequate education
5. Poor recreation facilities and programs
6. Ineffectiveness of the political structure and grievance mechanisms

Third Level

7. Disrespectful white attitudes
8. Discriminatory administration of justice
9. Inadequacy of federal programs
10. Inadequacy of municipal services
11. Discriminatory consumer and credit practices
12. Inadequate welfare programs [Kerner, 1968: 8, 143-157; compare Platt, 1971; Boesel and Rossi, 1971; Fogelson, 1968].

In 1981, the Scarman report on the first wave of British riots (April, Brixton) found most of the same issues housing, education, welfare, municipal services — although it laid most stress on unemployment and policing issues. In Miami, too, jobs and police practices were among the vital grievances. It begins to look as if the events of the last two years have not been a new pattern of urban riot so much as a return to the old traditions of the 1960s.

This view seems confirmed if we examine the specific causes of different riots. In most cases, we find that serious violence was touched off by an apparently trivial incident. The massive disproportion between issue and response may be explained by the underlying grievances the specific incident seemed to point out. In the 1960s, such incidents might have included an arrest, a shooting, even a raid on a drinking club. However, the petty affair in question became a detonator because it led to protests against police behavior in general, as well as other social injustices. Kerner discerned a common "pattern of disorder": "discrimination, prejudice, disadvantaged conditions, intense and pervasive grievances, a series of tension-heightening incidents, all culminating in the eruption of disorder at the hands of youthful, politically-aware activists."

Such a description would be suitable for either Miami or the British riots. In Miami, for instance, the 1980 riot broke out on May 17, within hours of the acquittal of four police officers accused of killing a black businessman, Arthur McDuffie (*Prevention and Control of Urban Disorders,* 1980). McDuffie had been arrested for running red lights on his motorcycle. When caught by police, he had apparently been savagely beaten, while his injuries had been attributed to a road accident. In a sense, the rioting was aimed at avenging McDuffie, although the case aroused much deeper memories of grievances against the police. First, it raised the question of the physical safety and security of members of the black community against a force seen as brutal and racist. Second, the case suggested a thorough double standard in the administration of justice. Blacks were easily convicted and punished by the courts, but police officers or white authority figures seemed beyond the control of law or justice.

In the year before McDuffie died, other cases had raised these issues in the black community. In one, the Dade County Grand Jury had failed to indict an off-duty highway patrol officer following the shooting death of an unarmed young black man. Again, a Florida Highway Patrol Officer had escaped serious punishment by a county judge after sexually molesting a black child in his patrol car. In yet another incident, a wrong-house raid on the home of Nathaniel Lafleur, a black school teacher, by Metro-Dade County narcotics officers again failed to produce an indictment by the County Grand Jury. In striking contrast to such cases was the rapid and efficient conviction of a black community leader accused of diverting public funds to his own use; while ordinary black citizens comprised most of the raw material of the city's court and prison system. All these cases were "in the air" at the time of the McDuffie verdict. They help to explain why police and the justice system should have become the focus of deeper grievances such as housing and black unemployment (up to 40% in Dade County at the time of the riot). Finally, local grievances were compared with those of minorities elsewhere in the United States, seen and heard through the media. Before the riot, Miami residents could hear about the revival of the Ku Klux Klan, the Greensboro Killings, and police brutality cases in other cities such as Houston. All reports seemed to form one coherent picture — of racism, brutality, discrimination, and of black helplessness against political and economic authority.

The British riots usually began with similar incidents, such as arrests or police raids. The riot in Bristol in 1980 began like that in Detroit in 1967, with arrests in a quasi-legal social club. In July 1981, the Brixton fighting began with the arrest of a West Indian businessman; that in Liverpool began when a black motorcyclist was arrested on suspicion of theft. In some areas, the spark is relatively easy to understand. For instance, Asians were extremely sensitive to the danger of violent fascist attacks on their lives and property, and so the appearance of fascist groups in an Asian locality would certainly lead to violent resistance. This is how the Southall fighting began in July 1981. But why should an arrest on suspicion of theft cause so much fury? Here, we are back in a world very similar to that of Miami, or of the ghettos of the 1960s.

When the Kerner Commission elaborated on the offensive police practices so heavily to blame for the riots, it concentrated on verbal and physical abuse, abuse of blacks in police custody, and "nonexistent or inadequate channels for the redress of grievances against police" (Kerner: 146). These remarks can be applied wholesale to British cities in the 1980s. In the four or five years before the riots, many studies had found extensive evidence of racism and discrimination as part of the common currency of police life. In particular, this seemed to be institutionalized through the *sus* law, under which many young black people were charged and convicted with suspicious behavior (Humphry, 1972; McClure, 1980; Hall et al., 1978; Wyatt, 1980; New Statesman, January 30 and March 27, 1981; Howe, 1981; Hain et al., 1979). Brutality, the planting of evidence, and the forcing of confessions were equally apparent and were equally unlikely to result in disciplinary action against the police. Scandals focused on cases like Liddle Towers, arrested for a trivial offense in Newcastle-on-Tyne and apparently beaten to death in much the same way as McDuffie; or on Blair Peach, killed in an antifascist demonstration in Southall. In each case, the police officers responsible for the deaths of these (white) men were known with fair certainty, yet no action was taken. Where Miami had McDuffie, LaFleur, Heath, and other scandals, Britain had Liddle Towers and Blair Peach.

Liverpool is an excellent example of such a perceived double standard—although as in the Towers case, many of the victims were white. Apart from its notorious racism, the Liverpool force has an appalling tradition of brutality and for violence inflicted on only trivial offenders, who had been picked up for after-hours drinking or merely acting suspiciously. Victims sometimes died, without either disciplinary action or even an inquiry into police behavior. One such scandal in 1974 involved a laborer, John Lannon; and a far better-known case in 1979 was that of Jimmy Kelly. In the Kelly case, an inquiry ensued—only to be blocked at every stage by the chief constable. The inquest verdict was "misadventure," despite such creative police inventions as attributing Kelly's broken ribs to an unsuccessful attempt at revival by heart massage. An internal police inquiry found no misconduct, but this was undertaken by a senior West Midlands officer who based his findings only on police evidence. About the time of Kelly's death, one group of officers was suspended for misconduct during a raid on a bar. Another group of four was disciplined for the arrest of one Peter Jeonney, who was beaten during arrest, "framed" for a crime, and wrongfully imprisoned for a three-year sentence.

Such misdeeds were largely suppressed in the media of the early 1970s, but they received increasing attention with the appearance of a local muckraking journal, the *Liverpool Free Press.* The police had an excellent record of avoiding public inquiry or reprimand: The fruits of this were not apparent until July 1981, when hundreds of officers were driven back by rioters chanting "There isn't only one Jimmy Kelly" (Whitaker, 1981; New Statesman, August 24 and November 30, 1979; June 6 and October 24, 1980; May 15 and July 10, 1981; McClure, 1980).

Charges of a double standard were made because the police seemed beyond censure. By contrast, draconian measures were taken against civilians involved in earlier riots (Southall 1979, Brixton 1980). One of the most painful grievances arose from the death of 13 blacks in a fire in Deptford (south London) in 1980. This was widely assumed to be a fascist attack, but was dismissed by authority as accidental. It combined all the major issues — fear of right-wing violence, the callousness of authority, the double standard, police indifference (or even sympathy) to the extreme right. Clearly, the Kerner "pattern of disorder" holds good for British events to a considerable degree. *To some extent,* if we change the names and dates, we can extract one common pattern for Watts in 1965, Detroit in 1967, Miami in 1980, or Liverpool in 1981 (Kettle and Hodges, 1982).

CONTRASTS

For all their superficial similarities, the various conflicts had deep differences — to such an extent that we can see the events of 1980-1981 as marking the beginning of a wholly new pattern of urban disorder. The most notable change can be summarized thus: The Kerner riots were mainly race riots with an element of class consciousness. By contrast (and oversimplifying), the Miami events were a race riot pure and simple; the British riots were equally clearly manifestations of class protest.

To compare Miami in 1980 with Liverpool or Brixton in 1981 is to compare two different worlds. In Miami, the riot began with savage attacks by blacks against whites, with random killing, torture, and mutilation. Some whites began to respond with equally indiscriminate attacks on blacks. In Liverpool, rioters were a thoroughly desegregated body, perhaps 50%-60% white, and this was typical of British events. Overwhelmingly, the rioters were drawn from the young working class of a particular area. In Brixton, this meant that rioters were mainly black, but there were no attacks on whites *as whites.* Rioters spoke the language of class, not race; and in Liverpool, they showed a remarkable level of political consciousness. Buildings like the Racquet Club were destroyed because they were the resort of the rich; a bank was destroyed because it was known to be the branch of a firm that invested in South Africa; and the riot was temporarily suspended while the crowds helped evacuate an old people's home endangered by fire.

To a surprising extent, it was Liverpool rather than Miami which was here following the traditional American pattern. Although the ghetto rioters of the 1960s had rarely showed so much ability to discriminate in choosing political targets, they were not primarily antiwhite. In some areas in the 1960s, 15% of arrestees were white, as were several of those killed as "snipers." In Miami, matters had changed totally by 1980. The rioters had formed the perception that their sufferings at the hands of the police were only part of a broader scheme to keep blacks permanently at the base of society. Particular hatred was felt of whites as such, and especially of new immigrants who seemed to be moving into successful positions over the heads of the existing black underclass. The news media paid a great deal of attention to Southeast Asian "boat people," who were not a significant presence in Miami. However, new Cuban and Hispanic refugees were a noticeable force, and these were the preferred targets of rioters.

The background to this migration can be seen as a result of official mismanagement. In April 1980, President Jimmy Carter talked about "open arms and an open heart," and invited some 125,000 Cubans (through Mariel), and some 7,200 Haitians to arrive in Florida; most settled for at least eight months in the Dade County area. At the time of the riots, the roughly 100,000 Cuban and 35,000 Haitian refugees were demanding some type of social service from Dade County coffers. Much of this relief came at the expense of the needy black community.

This wave of mainly illegal immigration caused a great deal of anger throughout the Dade County community but particularly among Dade blacks. In an extensive survey completed after the riots by the Local Behavioral Science Research Institute in conjunction with the *Miami Herald,* some 90% of 500 black citizens questioned agreed that the black community had been seriously hurt by the influx of Cubans and was a contributing factor to the riots. Almost two out of three respondents said their hatred of whites was a major factor in the disturbance.

As unemployment grew and welfare seemed about to be cut, it was easy to blame the other communities for taking away the small share of the spoils blacks had won in the past two decades. Miami blacks had particular grievances here, but police authorities remain well aware of the similar situations that could lead to comparable unrest in Sunbelt cities like Houston, Atlanta, Tampa, and Los Angeles (as well as the old grievances of Newark or Cleveland). For all its distinctiveness, Miami was not unique, and it seems as if other cities could imitate it by combining intercommunity violence with antipolice protest.

America has tended to take one direction in the years since Kerner; Britain has moved in another. The new riots of 1980-1981 in both countries can be seen as ultimately a response to unemployment, depression, and the lack of hope that government would be willing or be able to provide a solution. But who should be blamed for decline? The two countries took very different courses, partly reflecting underlying political characteristics. Americans tended to emphasize ethnic problems; the British found a solution in class terms, and blamed the social status quo.

But matters might have been very different. In the new pattern of mass structural unemployment that has beset Western economics in the last ten years, there has been a great temptation to find scapegoats for decline. In Miami, it was the new Cuban refugees. In Britain, it might very easily have been nonwhites in general. Until recently, there were predictions that the response to unemployment and poverty in British cities might have been very like what happened in Miami in 1980, but with blacks as victims rather than activists. Throughout the 1970s, the extreme right frequently noted that the number of unemployed in Britain was almost exactly the number of the nonwhite population; and they protested particularly about continuing immigration. In 1972 and 1976, new waves of immigrants were the focus for racial violence similar to that of Miami—although on a far smaller scale. In 1974, a secret government report warned of an imminent "white backlash" against colored communities, leading to interracial fighting (Guardian Weekly, April 19, 1981). As late as February 1981, a Labour M.P. remarked of widespread bitterness about mass unemployment: "The one thing we haven't seen, thank God, is a major racial explosion. The easiest people to blame would be the immigrants" (Time, February 16, 1981). As

we have shown, the events of that summer would show that his perception was far from reality.

EXPLANATIONS

In a sense, it is easier to explain the violence in Miami than that in
Britain, and why they should be so different from the Kerner pattern.
The riots of the 1960s took place against a much more favorable
economic background—in which, for example, 20% youth unemployment was regarded as terrifyingly high, as against the 50% or 60% common today. Also, there was more change of government intervention
to ameliorate poverty than under the monetarist policies of the last few
years. In consequence, greater violence might be expected to arise from
despair and helplessness, and it is not surprising that it should have been
directed against other communities. Why was Britain different?

To explain this, it is necessary to look at British social and political
developments over the last 15 years, the long-term context of the riots.
In that time, we would argue that Britain underwent a crisis far deeper
than that of the United States, which helps to explain the nature of the
unrest in 1980-1981. Several major factors should be isolated:

(1) A widespread perception of inevitable and growing economic decline,
    based on financial crises and mass unemployment—up to 13% by 1981
    (Taylor, 1981; Hall et al., 1978; Glyn and Harrison, 1980).
(2) The view of government as incompetent, callous, and scandal-ridden.
    Ideological politics and parties lost much of support, while scandals
    (Thorpe, Poulson, Maudling, the Wilson Honors list) discredited tradi-
    tional respect for government and authority.
(3) A belief that this same corrupt and inefficient system was attempting
    to become more arbitrary and repressive (Ackroyd, et al., 1977; Hall et
    al., 1978; Bunyan, 1977 and 1981-2). How long would it be before Ulster-
    style policing came to London or Birmingham?
(4) Structural problems within the justice system—a crisis of authority within
    the police, and charges of corruption and brutality. A crisis in the prisons,
    the double standard in the courts (Fitzgerald, 1977; Cox et al., 1977; Mark,
    1978; Holdaway, 1979).

In consequence of the political and economic crisis that began in the
early 1970s, Britain (like much of Europe) acquired a youth underclass,
with their own nihilistic subculture based on gangs, football, and rock

music. This subculture was deeply alienated from the police and from governments, but it was likely to be won over to new politics offering a radical alternative. It was these people who would provide the components of a future riot, either of the Miami type (intercommunity violence) or of the Liverpool variety (nonracial unity against the police and authority).

Why one type rather than the other? While youth suffered from some of the same police abuses as blacks, at first it seemed that they would accept the views of the extreme right. In 1975 and 1976, many young people were won over by extreme right-wing movements like the National Front, and football crowds chanted fascist political slogans. At that point, it seemed likely that the Miami pattern would hold good in Britain, and if riots had occurred in 1976 they would indeed have been race riots, of white against black (Walker, 1977).

However, matters changed totally between 1975 and 1978, as a result of left-wing "anti-Nazi" campaigns. By the skillful use of front organizations and a near takeover of "New Wave" music, the new youth culture was gained for the political Left. Soon, football crowds were more likely to be heard using chants that were political, even anarchist. Some chanted the names of Jimmy Kelly or Liddle Towers at the police; others referred to a mass-murderer of the 1960s when they said "Harry Roberts is our friend/he kills policemen." Rock music now became a vehicle of left-wing libertarian rhetoric among disaffected youth. Songs attacked government corruption and repression, police brutality, and frame-ups; and a movement called "Rock Against Racism" regularly attracted over 100,000 people to events like free carnivals.

By 1977, it became impossible for the extreme right to mobilize young sympathizers or even to appear in street demonstrations. The National Front was totally discredited, and this was reflected in election results. In communities where the NF had been winning 8%-12% of the vote in local elections in the spring of 1976 or 1977, by 1978 they were down to 3%-4%. In parliamentary elections, the trend was equally marked. In 1974, NF candidates had regularly won 3% or 4% of votes, and had sometimes achieved 8%-10%, raising the party's hopes of eventual national power. In May 1979, the same constituencies rarely provided the NF with more than a 1% share. With the failure of their respectable image, the extreme right often turned to random racial terror, arson, and provocation; from the broad populist appeal of the NF to the narrow Nazi sectarianism of the British Movement.

So by 1978, British politics had been wholly changed. In 1975, racial divisions threatened community violence. By 1979, they even promised a gleam of hope for the young. As the slump deepened, blacks came into more frequent conflict with the police (the Notting Hill riot of 1976 marked the first of a series of battles). In so doing, they were beginning to provide white youth with a potential outlet for despair and frustration. After the anti-Nazi campaigns, it would be very difficult to attempt to blame members of other races for growing economic problems. When riots came, they would be political class riots, with all that implied for their nature and impact.

SOLUTIONS

We have tried to suggest that the Kerner Commission's explanations for the causes of riots were substantially right. At least, they worked well in explaining disorder in very different settings over a decade later. What has changed is that some of the main causes—those of primary intensity, like unemployment—have become far worse and are likely to continue to deteriorate. As a result, riots have recurred on at least as serious a level of the 1960s, and they too are likely to grow. What has changed is the political content of those riots: Britain probably leads the way in Europe in moving toward riots that are oriented toward class and ideology; Miami seems to suggest that American disorders will become more truly race riots, internecine conflicts of appalling ferocity.

This view is doubly pessimistic. It suggests that the ideological riots likely from the politicized young underclass of Europe will be a serious threat at least to public order, and perhaps to the security of the state. We are not looking at the middle-class dissidents of the 1968 student risings, but of the desperately poor, hopeless, and determined. For America, the prospect seems to be one of relatively nonpolitical but nonetheless savage violence. Also, this would be violence of the kind that inspires counterviolence and tends to make communities arm against each other. Already in Miami, white and Hispanic vigilante groups made a brief appearance in 1980.

What can be done to prevent these disturbing prospects becoming reality? Again, we look to the Kerner Commission. If it was so accurate in assessing the causes of the riots, presumably its solutions should be worth consideration. It recommended that massive government effort be directed to overcoming discrimination and racism; and that an enormous policy of social reconstruction be undertaken in the cities. This would include reforms in education, housing, and welfare, but central to the whole scheme was the attack on unemployment. Kerner urged the creation of a million new jobs in three years, which would halve the existing unemployment level. After all, "the pervasive effect of these conditions [unemployment and underemployment] on the racial ghetto is inextricably linked to the problem of civil disorder" (Kerner, 1968: 413-414).

In 1981, Lord Scarman's report on the British riots cited the Kerner recommendations on massive social reform, and added approvingly, "These words are as true of Britain today as they have been provided by subsequent events to be true of America" (Scarman, 1982: 136). But looking back on such suggestions today produces something of a sense of unreality — not to mention increduality that Scarman should still think them feasible. Kerner was writing at a time when national United States unemployment stood at 3.8%, not the 10% or more that characterizes the United States in 1983, or the 13% or more Britain suffers from. The level of black unemployment Kerner regarded as likely to lead to ghetto disorders is now, roughly, the level of *white* unemployment in many areas. In light of the spread of new technology and the further decline of traditional industries, it is widely predicted that real unemployment in Western countries might reach 20% by the end of the 1980s. It is inconceivable that Kerner suggestions here could be accepted even as *aspirations,* still less as hard policies. If this fundamental component fails, surely the other social programs fall with it. Kerner's recommendations were written at a time of a broad assumption about continued economic growth, one on which government spending levels depended. Those assumptions have — since the crisis of 1973-1975 — proved totally false. In the context of the 1970s and 1980s, the liberal demands of Kerner seem like revolutionary slogans. It may be that riots both recent and imminent herald a social crisis that could be resolved *only* by massive redistributions of wealth and power (Glyn and Harrison, 1980; Cloward and Piven, 1975; Piven and Cloward, 1971; Jenkins and Potter, 1982).

If, as we assume, this does not occur in the near future, what other solutions or stopgaps can be found? Can anything be salvaged from Kerner? The only answer would appear to lie in changing the police role, a suggestion that places an enormous (and perhaps unfair) responsibility on law enforcement officials. In summary, Kerner recommended that American forces needed to change their ghetto image of an army of occupation, and the extent in which they have succeeded in this might be indicated by the relative tranquility of United States cities in the 1970s. Here, British forces have an immense amount to learn—in avoiding gratuitous insult to young, poor, or black members of the public, in learning not to overreact to civil disorder, in the abolition of the intensive policing campaigns in black areas (the last such effort, "Swamp 81," was the direct cause of the Brixton riot of April 1981, which left 279 officers injured).

This failure to learn may also be observed by comparing the tactics used by British and Miami police in 1980-1981. The British police used the tactics of confrontation throughout 1981, with the consequent injuries and damage to their public image. Indeed, their tactics give the rioters an opportunity to vent their anger and frustration on convenient targets. Conversely, in Miami, the police were relegated primarily to perimeter duty and in very few instances confronted by rioters (the exception being scattered attempted rescue of white citizens who became trapped in inner Liberty City). The results of these tactics were that not one officer suffered an injury that required treatment. The rioters, however, chiefly attacked civilians and private property. There were few citizens injured in the rare citizen-police confrontations. Again, despite the accessibility of firearms, no officer was wounded by sniper fire. The attitude of the police was summed up by one sergeant: "We shouldn't do anything... we can return later and clean up."

So the police role is significant in determining both the outbreak of rioting and the course it will follow. But to return to the question of causation, even if obvious provocations are avoided, we are not, of course, suggesting that police reforms in themselves could cure or prevent riots. The police would be controlling areas in a time of declining employment, rising poverty and crime, and probably cuts in welfare and social services (Wright, 1981). All they could do is reduce areas of possible provocation to a minimum. Here, the largest single area of change would seem to be that of the double standard. It must become possible to create greater public trust in complaints procedures against the police, and a belief that police malfeasance will be severely punished. Of course, there are enormous obstacles to such a change, not least that variety of police professionalism that forbids testifying against a fellow officer. But the alternative to some such change is a repetition of the savage antipolice rioting in 1980-1981.

Even if the attitudes of ordinary officers are hard to alter, higher authorities might be expected to lead reform. In May 1982, a case was reported in north London when a black couple had their house searched by the police, they were assaulted and insulted for little reason, and their complaints resulted in a number of malicious prosecutions being brought against them. A judge awarded them substantial damages; but the police refused to take any disciplinary action against the officers involved, "because no complaint against any individual officer had been received." By coincidence, the week this case was decided was also one in which renewed riots occurred in Brixton and Liverpool, and in which riot squad officers were accused of excessive brutality in another black area of London (Guardian Weekly, May 2, 1982). Everything conspires to suggest that in Britain at least, Kerner's recommendations for the police as well as the economy had gone totally unheard. If even the lessons of 1981 had gone unheeded, what else could influence policy?

CONCLUSION

Our conclusion must be pessimistic. The Kerner analysis of the riots as primarily a response to economic crisis and relative deprivation holds good; but the economic background has grown far, far worse, and improvement is not in sight in this century. Perhaps it is not to be hoped for within the present social or economic framework. Riots on the 1960s pattern are therefore very likely to recur in this decade—probably on at least as large a scale, and probably on new and more dangerous lines. Either they will be Miami riots, setting community against community, or they will be Liverpool riots, challenging governments and the social order. It is not an encouraging choice.

REFERENCES

NEWSPAPERS AND JOURNALS

Material on the riots of 1980 and 1981 was gathered from a number of sources other than those listed in the text. These included the following:

Birmingham Post	*Police*
Daily Telegraph	*Police Magazine*
Guardian Weekly	*The Progressive*

International Socialism
Leveller
Miami Herald
Nation
New Leader
New Society
New Statesman
Newsweek
New York Times

Race Today
Race and Class
Searchlight
Socialist Worker
Sunday Times
Time
US News and World Report
Village Voice

BOOKS AND ARTICLES

ACKROYD, C. et al. (1977) The Technology of Political Control. London: Harmondswirth.

ALLMAN, T. D. (1981) "Pomp and discretion." Harpers, November.

BOESEL, D. and P. M. ROSSI [eds.] (1971) Cities Under Siege: An Anatomy of the Ghetto Riots 1964-68. New York: Basic Books.

BRIDGES, L. (1981) "Keeping the lid on." Race and Class 23, 2-3.

BUNYAN, T. (1981) "The police against the people." Race and Class 23, 2-3.

— — — (1977) History and Practice of the Political Police in Britain. London: Quartet.

CLOWARD, R. A. and F. F. PIVEN (1975) The Politics of Turmoil. New York: Vintage.

COX, B. et al. (1977) The Fall of Scotland Yard. London: Harmondsworth.

FEAGIN, J. R. and H. HAHN (1973) Ghetto Revolt: The Politics of Violence in American Cities. New York: Macmillan.

FITZGERALD, M. (1977) Prisoners in Revolt. London: Harmondsworth.

FOGELSON, R. (1968) "From resentment to confrontation: the police, the Negroes and the outbreak of the 1960s riots." Political Science Quarterly (June): 217-247.

GELB, N. (1981) "The roots of Britain's riots." New Leader (August 10).

GILROY, P. (1981) "You can't fool the youths..." Race and Class 23, 2-3.

GLYN, A. and J. HARRISON (1980) The British Economic Disaster. London: Pluto Press.

GRAHAM, H. D. and T. R. GURR (1969) Violence in America. New York: Signet.

GURR, T. R. et al. (1977) The Politics of Crime and Conflict. Beverly Hills, CA: Sage.

HAIN, P. et al. (1979) Policing the Police. London: John Calder.

HALL, S. et al. (1978) Policing the Crisis. London: Macmillan.

— — — (1981) "Summer in the city." New Socialist (Sept./Oct.).

HARMAN, C. (1981) "The summer of 1981." International Socialism 14.

HOLDAWAY, S. [ed.] (1979) The British Police. Beverly Hills, CA: Sage.

HOWE, D. (1981) "Bobby to Babylon." Race Today 23, 2-3.

HUMPHRY, D. (1972) Police Power and Black People. London: Panther.

JAMES, D. (1979) "Police—Black relations" in S. Holdaway (ed.) British Police. Beverly Hills, CA: Sage.

JENKINS, P. and G. W. POTTER (1982) "The dominance of authority." Contemporary Crises.

Kerner (1968) Report of the National Advisory Commission on Civil Disorders. New York: Bantam.

KETTLE, M. and L. HODGES (1982) Uprising. London: Pan.

KUSHNICK, L. (1981) "Parameters of British and North American racism." Race and Class 23, 2-3.

McCLURE, J. (1980) Spike Island. London.

MARK, SIR R. (1978) In the Office of Constable. London: Collins.

PIVEN, F. F. and R. A. CLOWARD (1971) Regulating the Poor. New York: Vintage.

PLATT, A. (1971) The Politics of Riot Commissions. New York: Macmillan.

Prevention and Control of Urban Disorders: Issues for the 1980s (1980) Washington, DC: U.S. Department of Justice, LEAA.

Scarman (1982) The Brixton Disorders 10-12 April, 1981: Report of an Inquiry (Cmnd 8427). London: HMSO.

SIVANANDAN, A. (1981) "From resistance to rebellion." Race and Class 23, 2-3.

TAYLOR, I. (1981) Law and Order. London: Macmillan.

WALKER, M. (1977) The National Front. London: Collins.

WHITAKER, B. (1981) News Limited. London: Minority Press Group.

WRIGHT, K. [ed.] (1981) The Criminal Justice System in a Declining Economy. Cambridge, MA: Oegelschlager, Gunn and Hain.

WYATT, J. (1980) "Law and order British style." Nation (July 5).

Ineke Haen Marshall

University of Nebraska, Omaha

6

THE WOMEN'S MOVEMENT AND
FEMALE CRIMINALITY
IN THE NETHERLANDS

The women's movement has been blamed for many of society's ills; it is held responsible, among other things, for the increased criminality among females. Starting with the publication of *Sisters in Crime* (Adler, 1975) and *Women and Crime* (Simon, 1975), the belief that changes in the traditional roles of women are directly responsible for increased female crime rates has become a virtual truism. Steffensmeier (1978: 571) summarized the common theme linking the different variants of the emancipation hypothesis[1] as follows: "Sex differences in levels of crime diminish as men and women move toward greater equality in their rights and privileges."

One particularly popular image of the "new female criminal" is that of an aggressive woman, invading the traditionally male domain of violent and major property crime (i.e., murder, robbery, burglary). This is the impression conveyed by Adler (1975), who foresees a future upsurge in the number of women involved in violent as well as major property crimes. Recent empirical studies, however, have begun to challenge the notion that women are increasingly emulating male criminal career patterns (see, for example, Steffensmeier, 1978, 1980). Instead, it seems that female criminal involvement has mainly increased for property crimes such as fraud, forgery, and larceny-theft. Such findings are consistent with Simon's (1975: 47) opportunity theory of female crime: "Women are committing those types of crimes that their participation in the labor force provides them with greater opportunities to commit than they have had in the past."

87

This chapter aims to evaluate the emancipation hypothesis by analyzing changes in female arrests in The Netherlands for the period of 1958-1977. Specifically, the analysis attempts to answer two questions. First, has there been an increase in rates of violent and property crime for females in The Netherlands? Second, has the gap between males and females in rates of violent and property crime decreased in The Netherlands over the period 1958-1977?

METHODOLOGY

The data for the analysis are derived from official arrest statistics published monthly by the Dutch Central Bureau of Statistics. There is no need to elaborate here on the problems of reliability and validity of official crime statistics. These problems have been discussed extensively elsewhere (see, for example, Steffensmeier, 1978). Important for our purposes is the conclusion that "we are reasonably safe in using. . . arrest data for purposes of examining the relative differences in. . . crime levels between males and females over a given time period" (Steffensmeier, 1978: 570). Steffensmeier refers to FBI statistics; however, there is no reason to believe that his argument is not equally appropriate for Dutch crime statistics.

Two sets of arrest data are presented: (1) sex-specific arrest rates per 100,000 for females and males between the ages of 12 and 64[2] and (2) the percentage that females contribute to the total (male and female) arrest rate. These percentages enable comparisons of male and female arrest rates and allow us to determine whether the *relative* gap in male and female crime levels has narrowed or widened (see Steffensmeier, 1980).

In addition to annual rates for the period of 1958-1977, average rates and average percentages have also been calculated for the four consecutive five-year periods: 1958-1962, 1963-1967, 1968-1972, and 1973-1977. The first two periods (1958-1962 and 1963-1967) may be referred to as the prefeminist era; the 1968-1972 period represents the early beginnings of the feminist movement; and in the fourth period (1973-1977) the feminist movement had begun to gain a modest following in The Netherlands. If the women's movement has indeed had an effect on female criminality, then we would expect that the relative gap between male and female crime levels shows a significant narrowing in the later periods under study. The use of averages has the additional advantage of smoothing the effects of erratic annual fluctuations which provides a more stable measure than the rate for one single year.

Data on the following eight crime categories are used: (1) crimes against life *(tegen het leven);* (2) physical abuse *(mishandeling);* (3) crimes against public order and authority *(tegen de openbare orde en gezag);* (4) vandalism *(vernieling);* (5) fraud *(bedrog);* (6) embezzlement *(verduistering);* (7) simple theft *(eenvoudige diefstal);* and (8) shoplifting *(winkeldiefstal).* The Dutch legal definitions of vandalism, fraud, embezzlement, simple theft, and shoplifting are quite similar to those employed in the United States, but this is not the case for the crimes against life, physical abuse, and crimes against public order and authority.

Crimes involving personal violence are defined rather ambiguously in The Netherlands. As a rule of thumb, the more serious cases of assault tend to be classified as crimes against life, and the less serious cases are usually grouped under the label of physical assault. Crimes against life cover a wide range of assaultive behavior, ranging from homicide, attempted homicide, manslaughter, and aggravated assault to assault resulting in relatively minor physical injuries to the victim. Quite peculiarly, the classification scheme does not allow one to distinguish homicide from other forms of assault. Furthermore, even the less serious category of physical assault may include cases where the victim died of his or her injuries. It should be pointed out that the bulk of the cases in both categories involves injuries of a relatively minor nature.[3]

Crimes involving the use of physical violence against other persons are not the only instances where definitional idiosyncracies exist. Crimes against public order and authority also cover a hodgepodge of varied behaviors, from insult to public authorities, disturbance of domestic peace, refractoriness, interference with public officials, to violence against persons or property in conjunction. Thus, crimes against public order and authority include different forms of civil disobedience and political violence such as those manifested in antigovernment demonstrations, squatting incidents, and student actions in several Dutch cities and towns.

The analysis is divided into two parts. The first part focuses on so-called masculine crimes that

> require stereotyped male behavior, involving masculine skills and techniques and are usually committed by males. Commonly, they are defined as crimes involving physical strength and daring, elements of coercion

and confrontation with the victim, and/or specialized skills [Steffensmeier, 1980: 1093].

Specifically, the following crimes are defined as "masculine" for purposes of the analysis: (1) against life; (2) physical abuse; (3) against public order and authority; and (4) vandalism. The "aggressive" version of the emancipation hypothesis suggests that women's participation in these crimes should have increased at a faster rate than males'. The second part of the analysis addresses the "opportunity" version of emancipation theory by analyzing changes in the property crimes of (1) fraud, (2) embezzlement, (3) simple theft, and (4) shoplifting.

CHANGES IN FEMALE INVOLVEMENT
IN MASCULINE CRIME, 1958-1977

Violence Against Persons

Examination of Table 6.1 shows that the female rate for crimes against life has incresed very slightly since 1973. The average rate for crimes against life for females in the period 1973-1977 is 1.3 as compared to an average female arrest rate of less than 1 per 100,000 females in the preceding 15 years (see Table 6.2). On the other hand, the data in Table 6.1 also show that the gap between males and females for crimes against life has gradually increased over the 20-year time span under examination. The statistics indicate a gradual but consistent decrease of the relative importance of female arrests for the total arrest rate for crimes against life. For example, in 1958, men were six times more likely to be arrested for crimes against life than females; in 1977, the odds for a male arrest over a female have increased to 14 against 1.

Somewhat comparable patterns are found for the crime of physical assault (Tables 6.1 and 6.2). Examination of female crime rates shows a consistent decrease in female arrests for physical assault; the arrest rate in 1977 (12.9) is about one-third of the comparable rate in 1958 (36.8). Male arrest rates for physical assault have remained relatively stable over the years; as a matter of fact, the 1958 rate (199.7) is very close to the 1977 rate (198). It is apparent from Tables 6.1 and 6.2 that the gap between males and females for physical assault has gradually widened, mostly as a result of declining involvement in female arrests for physical assault.

A personal violence index was constructed by combining the arrests for crimes against life with those for physical assault (see Tables 6.1 and

TABLE 6.1 Masculine Crime Arrest Rates per 100,000 for Females and Males, and Percentage of Female Contribution to Total Arrest Rates*

Year	Against Life			Physical Assault			Violence Against Persons Index**		
	Female	Male	% Contribution	Female	Male	% Contribution	Female	Male	% Contribution
1977	1.7	22.3	7.1	12.9	198.0	6.1	14.6	220.3	6.2
1976	1.4	23.7	5.6	12.8	197.6	6.1	14.2	221.3	6.0
1975	0.9	20.1	4.3	11.2	177.3	5.9	12.1	197.4	5.8
1974	1.1	20.6	5.1	11.7	175.5	6.2	12.8	196.1	6.1
1973	1.2	18.2	6.2	12.9	194.9	6.2	14.1	213.1	6.2
1972	0.7	15.2	4.4	13.4	185.4	6.7	14.1	200.6	6.6
1971	0.7	13.2	5.0	14.0	179.1	7.2	14.7	192.3	7.1
1970	0.8	12.0	6.3	14.1	181.6	7.2	14.9	193.6	7.1
1969	1.0	10.5	8.7	18.0	188.1	8.7	19.0	198.6	8.7
1968	0.8	9.7	7.6	18.4	181.2	9.2	19.2	190.9	9.1
1967	0.9	10.5	7.9	18.0	184.6	8.9	18.9	195.1	8.8
1966	0.7	8.2	7.9	16.7	187.1	8.2	17.4	195.3	8.2
1965	0.9	8.3	9.4	19.9	182.9	9.8	20.8	191.2	9.8
1964	1.0	7.9	11.2	22.7	191.8	10.6	23.7	199.7	10.6
1963	1.0	6.7	13.0	22.3	180.9	11.0	23.3	187.6	11.0
1962	0.7	6.9	9.2	24.3	181.1	11.8	25.0	188.0	11.7
1961	0.5	6.4	7.2	31.5	197.3	13.8	32.0	203.7	13.6
1960	1.1	6.8	13.9	33.2	216.9	13.3	34.3	223.7	13.3
1959	0.6	6.3	8.7	36.6	205.1	15.1	37.2	211.4	15.0
1958	1.0	6.0	14.3	36.8	199.7	15.6	37.8	205.7	15.5

*The formula for computing the % female contribution to total arrest rates is $\dfrac{\text{female rate}}{(\text{male} + \text{female rate})} \times 100$.

**The Violence Against Persons Index is a combination of Crimes Against Life and Physical Assault.

TABLE 6.2 Masculine Crime Arrest Rates (averages) per 100,000 for Females and Males, and Percentage of Female Contribution (averages) to Total Arrest Rates*

Period	Against Life			Physical Assault			Personal Violence Index**			Against Public Order and Authority			Vandalism			Combined Masculine Crime Index***		
	Female	Male	% Contribution	Female	Male	% Contribution	Female	Male	% Contribution	Female	Male	% Contribution	Female	Male	% Contribution	Female	Male	% Contribution
1973-1977	1.3	21.0	5.7	12.3	188.7	6.1	13.6	209.7	6.1	7.7	135.5	5.4	7.0	181.1	3.8	28.3	526.2	5.1
1968-1972	0.8	12.1	6.4	15.6	183.1	7.8	16.4	195.2	7.7	5.7	108.4	5.0	4.8	121.4	3.8	26.8	425.0	6.0
1963-1967	0.9	8.3	9.9	19.9	185.5	9.7	20.8	193.8	9.7	4.9	81.9	5.7	4.7	107.4	4.3	30.4	383.1	7.4
1958-1962	0.8	6.5	10.7	32.5	200.0	13.9	33.3	206.5	13.8	5.9	77.2	7.1	6.1	88.6	6.4	45.2	372.3	10.8

*The formula for computing the % contribution to total arrest rates is $\dfrac{\text{female rate}}{(\text{male} + \text{female rate})} \times 100$.

**The Personal Violence Index is a combination of Crimes Against Life and Physical Assault.
***The Combined Masculine Crime Index is a combination of Crimes Against Life, Physical Assault, Crimes Against Public Order and Authority, and Vandalism.

6.2). The personal violence index (PVI) shows that the rate for overall female involvement in personal violence has gradually decreased over the 20-year period, with the male rates showing a relatively stable pattern. In The Netherlands, as in most other societies, personal violence has remained a male phenomenon par excellence; in 1977 males were about 16 times more likely than women to be arrested for a violent crime against a person.

Crimes Against Public Order and Authority

The rates for female involvement in crimes against the public order do not show a clear pattern, at least not in the first 15 years (1958-1973) under study (see Table 6.1). The rates fluctuate between a low of 4.1 (1967) and a high of 6.6 (1960). The average rate for the 1958-1962 period (5.9) is about the same as the average rate for the 1968-1972 period (5.7; see Table 6.2). A slight upward trend in female arrest rates starting in 1973 (7.4) appears to persist till 1977 (8.2). On the other hand, the male involvement in crimes against public order and authority has doubled in the 20-year period (72.4 in 1958; 159.8 in 1977). This probably explains why the involvement of females relative to males for this type of crime has decreased slightly over the time period under examination. For instance, in the 1958-1962 period, 14 males were arrested for every 1 female apprehended, but in the 1973-1977 period, the ratio has increased to 18 (males) to 1 (female).

Vandalism

The pattern for vandalism is comparable to what was observed for crimes against the public order and authority (see Tables 6.1 and 6.2). The first 15 years (1958-1972) do not show a clear pattern: The rates fluctuate between a low of 4.2 (1963) and a high of 6.3 (1961). Interestingly, the average rate for the period 1958-1962 (6.1) is higher than the comparable rates for two later periods (4.7 for 1963-1967 and 4.8 for 1968-1972). A minor upward trend begins in 1973 (6.1) and continues until 1977 (8.5). The relative gap between males and females decreased slightly over the first 10 years under study (from a 7.1% female contribution in 1958 to a 3.7% female contribution in 1967) but has remained virtually constant during the last 10 years (fluctuating between a low of 3.5% female contribution in 1977 and a high of 4.0% female contribution in 1970). It appears, then, that the involvement of males in vandalism has increased at approximately the same rate as the female involvement, at least during the last 10 years under study (1968-1977). Vandalism has remained a very masculine activity in The Netherlands: Female involvement in vandalism relative to male involvement has actually decreased by 50% since 1958.

Combined Masculine Crime Index

The figures for the combined masculine crime index (CMCI) presented in Tables 6.1 and 6.2 summarize the general trends concerning female involvement in aggressive crimes in The Netherlands during the 1958-1977 period. Table 6.1 suggests that female arrests for masculine crimes have gradually decreased since 1958, but starting in 1973, a slight turn is apparent. However, the average rate for the 1973-1977 period (28.3) is still significantly lower than the average rate in 1958-1962 (45.2) and 1963-1967 (30.4). The percentage of female contribution to the overall arrest rate for masculine crimes shows a consistent decrease. For example, in the period 1958-1962, 1 out of every 10 arrests for this group of crimes involved a female; in the later period (1973-1977), females contributed only 5% to the overall arrest rates for masculine crimes.

CHANGES IN FEMALE INVOLVEMENT
IN PROPERTY CRIMES, 1958-1977

Fraud

The arrest rates for fraud for both females and males show a somewhat erratic pattern (see Tables 6.3 and 6.4). Female arrest rates for fraud were higher during the late 1950s-early 1960s (1958-1962: 8.1) and the late 1960s-early 1970s (1968-1972: 7.6) than in the mid-1960s (1963-1967: 5.0) and the mid-1970s (1973-1977: 4.9). A comparable pattern exists for male fraud arrests. Interestingly, the average female arrest rate for fraud for the 1973-1977 period (4.9) is lower than the rate for the early (1958-1962) period (8.1). This pattern also holds for male arrests (1958-1962: 58.4; 1973-1977: 40.5). Although it is hard to detect a pattern, it is safe to say that the gap between male and female arrests for fraud has not narrowed consistently over time. Rather, relatively fewer females were arrested for fraud in the last five years under study (percentage female contribution: 10.8) than in any of the three preceding five-year periods.

TABLE 6.3 Property Crime Arrest Rates per 100,000 for Females and Males, and Percentage of Female Contribution to Total Arrest Rates*

Year	Fraud			Embezzlement			Simple Theft			Shoplifting			Combined Property Crime Index**		
	Female	Male	% Contribution	Female	Male	% Contribution	Female	Male	% Contribution	Female	Male	% Contribution	Female	Male	% Contribution
1977	4.6	42.5	9.8	5.3	34.1	13.4	172.8	540.0	24.2	157.3	189.4	45.4	182.7	616.6	22.9
1976	4.8	38.3	11.1	5.2	34.5	13.1	174.8	512.8	25.4	160.7	180.8	47.0	184.8	585.6	24.0
1975	3.9	37.5	9.5	7.2	36.1	16.6	165.2	459.7	26.4	151.7	160.2	48.6	176.3	533.3	24.8
1974	4.8	36.1	11.7	6.2	36.7	14.5	148.2	472.6	23.9	136.5	141.9	49.0	159.2	545.4	22.6
1973	6.5	47.9	11.9	6.5	36.4	15.2	157.6	479.0	24.8	142.6	129.2	52.5	170.6	563.3	23.2
1972	6.6	47.8	12.1	6.4	42.4	13.1	153.0	467.7	24.6	137.5	125.9	52.2	166.0	557.9	22.9
1971	8.4	46.1	15.4	6.1	42.3	12.6	147.9	437.7	25.3	130.9	115.6	53.1	162.4	526.1	23.6
1970	7.5	49.8	13.1	6.7	44.7	13.0	144.1	416.8	25.7	126.1	108.2	53.8	158.3	511.3	23.6
1969	7.6	48.8	13.5	6.3	45.9	12.1	146.8	410.4	26.3	124.4	102.6	54.8	160.7	505.1	24.1
1968	8.1	47.3	14.6	6.6	45.6	12.6	134.0	418.1	24.3	107.7	92.3	53.8	148.7	511.0	22.5
1967	6.6	41.7	13.7	6.6	48.3	12.0	124.6	402.0	23.7	97.6	77.5	55.7	137.8	492.0	21.9
1966	4.6	36.8	11.1	6.4	46.2	12.2	125.4	385.3	24.6	99.2	82.0	54.7	136.4	468.3	22.6
1965	4.8	38.2	11.2	5.9	45.1	11.6	114.6	406.3	22.0	87.1	86.4	50.3	125.3	489.6	20.4
1964	4.4	35.0	11.2	7.4	50.7	12.7	118.6	438.2	21.3	87.5	86.5	50.3	130.4	523.9	19.9
1963	4.7	34.4	12.0	6.7	52.4	11.3	104.4	405.7	20.5	69.8	79.8	46.7	115.8	492.5	19.0
1962	6.0	39.0	13.3	7.1	54.7	11.5	97.2	401.0	19.5	62.3	69.6	47.2	110.3	494.7	18.2
1961	6.6	10.9	10.9	7.9	67.4	10.5	110.9	452.3	19.7	65.8	74.8	46.8	125.4	573.4	17.9
1960	9.0	59.3	13.2	7.1	73.9	8.8	106.9	446.4	19.3	57.7	65.6	46.8	123.0	579.6	17.5
1959	8.1	65.8	11.0	7.6	77.4	8.9	98.6	420.7	19.0	43.9	52.5	45.5	114.3	563.9	16.9
1958	11.0	74.1	12.9	9.1	88.4	9.3	95.8	439.6	17.9	43.1	54.2	44.3	115.9	602.1	16.1

*The formula for computing the % contribution to total arrest rates is $\dfrac{\text{female rate}}{(\text{female + male rate})} \times 100$.

**The Combined Property Crime Index is a combination of Fraud, Embezzlement, and Simple Theft.

TABLE 6.4 Property Crime Arrest Rates (averages) per 100,000 for Females and Males, and Percentage of Female Contribution (averages) to Total Arrest Rate*

Period	Fraud			Embezzlement			Simple Theft			Shoplifting			Combined Property Crime Index**		
	Female	Male	% Contribution	Female	Male	% Contribution	Female	Male	% Contribution	Female	Male	% Contribution	Female	Male	% Contribution
1973–1977	4.9	40.5	10.8	6.1	35.6	14.6	163.7	492.8	24.9	149.8	160.3	48.5	174.7	568.8	23.5
1968–1972	7.6	48.0	13.7	6.4	44.2	12.7	145.2	430.1	25.2	125.3	108.9	53.5	159.2	522.3	23.3
1963–1967	5.0	37.2	11.8	6.6	48.5	12.0	117.5	407.5	22.4	88.2	82.4	51.5	129.1	493.3	20.8
1958–1962	8.1	58.4	12.3	7.8	72.4	9.8	101.9	432.0	19.1	54.7	63.3	46.1	117.8	562.7	17.3

*The formula for computing the % contribution to total arrest rates is $\dfrac{\text{female rate}}{(\text{male} + \text{female rate})} \times 100$.

**The Combined Property Crime Index is a combination of Fraud, Embezzlement, and Simple Theft.

Embezzlement

Tables 6.3 and 6.4 indicate that male embezzlement rates have gradually decreased (1958: 88.4; 1977: 34.1). Female arrest rates for embezzlement show a similar gradual decline, albeit at a very moderate rate (1958: 9.1; 1977: 5.3). It appears that the gradual decrease of the gap between male and female arrests for embezzlement is due primarily to the fact that male arrests for embezzlement have decreased faster than female arrests for this particular offense. Thus, although female rates have decreased, their relative contribution to the overall embezzlement arrest rate has increased because of the even faster declining numbers of male arrests. Yet, declining male embezzlement arrest rates notwithstanding, embezzlement remains a masculine activity: In 1977, males were still about seven times more likely to be arrested for embezzlement than females.

Simple Theft

Female arrest rates for simple theft show a fairly consistent upward tendency: The female arrest rate of 95.8 per 100,000 (1958) almost doubled in the 20-year period under study (1977: 172.8 per 100,000; see Tables 6.3 and 6.4). The pattern for male arrest rates for simple theft is less clear, with perhaps the exception of the 1973-1977 period, which shows a modest increase over the preceding years (average rate of 492.8 compared to average rates of 432.0, 407.5, and 430.1, respectively). The percentage of females arrested for simple theft increased gradually during the first 10 years (1958: 17.9; 1967: 23.7); however, the percentage of female contribution to the overall arrest rate for simple theft remained fairly stable over the last 10 years. In the 1968-1977 period, the percentages fluctuate between a low of 23.9 in 1974 and a high of 26.4 in 1975. The average percentage female contribution for the 1973-1977 period (24.9%) is even slightly lower than that for the 1968-1972 period (25.2%). The statistics appear to indicate that during the 1968-1977 period, male arrests for simple theft increased at approximately the same rate as female arrests.

Shoplifting

The category of simple theft includes a variety of offenses, such as pickpocketing, purse snatching, bicycle theft, and shoplifting. Since shoplifting is considered a typical female crime, Tables 3.3 and 3.4 present separate statistics for this particular offense. Both male and female arrest rates show a consistent increase over the 20-year period. In the period 1958-1962, the female rate (54.6) is lower than the male rate (63.3), and a similar pattern is evident when looking at the 1973-1977 period (females: 149.8; males: 160.3). In the interim 10-year period (1963-1972), however, female rates tend to be higher than those of males (with the exception of 1963). In the 1963-1972 period female arrests account for over half of all the arrests for shoplifting. Beginning in 1974, however, the relative importance of female arrests begins to show a gradual decline: the relative contribution of female arrests in 1977 (45.4%) is close to the 1959 figure (45.5%).

Combined Property Crime Index

Tables 6.3 and 6.4 summarize the statistics on property crime by combining the three categories of fraud, embezzlement, and simple theft in one index (CPCI). Female arrests for property crimes have gradually increased (from 115.9 in 1958 to 182.7 in 1977). Male rates show some fluctuations throughout the 1960s, and start to increase in the early 1970s. Females gained on their male counterparts between 1958 and 1968, but the relative gap between males and females concerning property crime arrests remained relatively stable over the last 10 years (1968-1977). In the 1958-1962 period, approximately one out of every six arrests for property offenses concerned a female suspect; during the 1968-1977 period, the arrest ratio for property theft decreased to about one female to three males.

SUMMARY OF FINDINGS

The first question our analysis was designed to address ("Has there been an increase in the male and female rates of masculine and property crime in the period, 1958-1977?") cannot be answered with a simple yes or no. That is, female arrests for personal violent crimes, fraud, and embezzlement decreased between 1958-1977, but more females were arrested for crimes against public order and authority, vandalism, and simple theft.

Analysis of changes in *absolute* arrest rates, however, does not address our second question: Has the gap between males and females for masculine and property crimes narrowed or widened in the 1958-1977 period? Indeed, in order to determine the impact of the women's movement on female criminality, we must examine the *relative* differences in crime levels between males and females over the time period 1958-1977.

Contrary to the predictions of the emancipation hypothesis, the relative gap between male and female arrests for masculine crimes increased (rather than decreased) between 1958-1977. In other words, relatively fewer females were arrested for crimes against life, physical assault, vandalism, and crimes against public order and authority in 1977 than in 1958. This is not to say, of course, that we observed a consistent pattern of decrease for these four crimes over the 20-year period. For example, arrest patterns for vandalism remained rather stable during the last decade (1968-1977), after an initial widening of the gap between males and females during the first 10 years (1958-1967) of observation. Further, the percentage of female arrests for crimes against public order and authority increased slightly over the 1973-1977 period, relative to the preceding (1968-1972) years. Only this last observation could possibly be interpreted as supportive of the emancipation hypothesis.

The findings with regard to property crime are somewhat more consistent with emancipation theory. For example, women's contribution to arrests for embezzlement became more important over the years. Yet, the absolute rate of female arrests for embezzlement consistently decreased during the 20-year period. Thus, females' "gain" for the crime of embezzlement is due to the even faster declining numbers of male arrests. The proportion of females arrested for fraud increased during the late 1960s; however, this increase started to level off during the mid-1970s, thus not providing strong supportive evidence for emancipation theory. A comparable pattern is noted for simple theft: During the first 10 years (1958-1967), the percentage of females among arrests for simple theft increased, but the last 10 years (1968-1977) showed a relatively stable male:female arrest ratio for this particular offense.

THE WOMEN'S MOVEMENT
IN THE NETHERLANDS

The emancipation hypothesis takes one proposition as self-evident: The women's movement has had a real and significant impact on the position of women in society. Since there is painfully little, if anything, that is self-evident, the remainder of this chapter examines some of the evidence regarding changes in gender roles in Dutch society between 1958 and 1977.

For most Western European countries, the period after World War II was characterized by rapidly increasing participation of women in the job market. The Netherlands was an exception to this general post-

World War II pattern: The participation of women in the labor market actually decreased between 1947 (24.4%) and 1960 (22.3%). Between 1960 and 1970, a time of economic prosperity and general shortage of workers, the number of working women increased somewhat. In 1971, 26% of the Dutch labor force was female. By 1977, the situation remained virtually unchanged: Of the Dutch labor force, 27% was female; nearly half of the female labor force was married; and two-thirds of the working women held full-time jobs (Berends and Boelmans-Kleinjan, 1979). These statistics clearly show that Dutch women have continued to play a relatively minor role in the world of salaried workers. Further, Dutch females have traditionally received fewer years of full-time education than males; hence, they tend to work in part-time, low-paying, low-status, low-security jobs (Meyer, 1977). Also, Dutch males typically attend more demanding schools, preparing them better for professional and academic careers. Though there have been modest gains in sexual equity over the last 20 years in the areas of employment and education, there remains significant gender inequality in Dutch public life.[4]

At least part of the impetus for change in female status has been the Dutch Women's Movement (Vrouwenbeweging). The women's movement in The Netherlands started in 1968 with the establishment of the action group Man-Woman-Society (Man-Vrouw-Maatschappij), a group emphasizing the limited job opportunities of women. The movement thereafter began to gain momentum. (For an analysis of this movement, see Weeda, 1981.) The 1970s witnessed the development of numerous consciousness-raising groups, women's cafes, women's shelters, women's telephone hotlines, women's publishing companies, and feminist magazines and television programs. Two universities developed women's studies programs, and a number of scholarly and polemic articles on women and feminism were published. Dutch activists have been quite successful in drawing attention to the secondary position of females in Dutch society — at least among the well-educated and upper classes. However, an important question remains: To what degree have the ideas of the women's movement actually "trickled down" to the average Dutch female? A 1979 study by Kooy addresses precisely this issue. He studied a sample of 1,119 Dutch women in order to determine their "emancipatory needs." Kooy found that the majority (75.5%) of the interviewed women were still satisfied with the allocation of tasks in the family, though these women accomplish a disproportionate share in household tasks. Kooy's study further shows that Dutch women still have rather traditional attitudes and values regarding their primary roles as mothers and wives. Only one-fourth of the respondents felt that women should both continue to work after marriage and not take time out for childrearing. Further, over 43% of the women indicated that in times of unemployment, women do not have the same right to a job as males.

CONCLUSION

Based on personal interviews with many Dutch experts on the family and the role of women, as well as my own observations as a sociologist living and growing up in The Netherlands, I am much persuaded by Kooy's conclusion: Dutch women's ideas concerning the central importance of the family have remained relatively unchanged. Dutch society has long placed much value in the traditional family, and the current women's movement has not appreciably changed this very central, cultural characteristic. As long as boys are still socialized to their future role as instrumental husbands and fathers, and girls are still prepared to be expressive wives and mothers, we may not expect a significant rise in the proportional involvement of females in masculine or property crimes — to wit the findings of the present study.

NOTES

1. The term "emancipation hypothesis" is used as an umbrella concept inclusive of all views explicitly or implicitly assuming a relationship between women's social position and female criminality.

2. Information on the proportion of the Dutch population (male and female) between the ages of 12 and 64 was obtained from two sources: (1) Bevolking van Nederland naar Geslacht, Leeftijd en Burgerlijke Staat 1830-1969 ('s-Gravenhage: Staatsuitgeverij), and (2) Criminele Statistiek 1960-1977 ('s-Gravenhage: Staatsuitgeverij).

3. For example, in Amsterdam only 28 murders took place between 1968 and 1970 (compared to 2,215 in Chicago for the same period). For the 1974-1976 period, Amsterdam had a total of 58 known homicides (compared to 2,576 homicides in Chicago for the same period). For a further comparison of homicide between Amsterdam and Chicago, see Block (1982).

4. For example, in 1958, 43% of all the 16-year-old boys went to school full-time, but only 30% of their female counterparts were full-time students. Ten years later (in 1967) the situation had not changed much: 60% of the 16-year-old boys and 46% of the 16-year-old girls attended school full-time. By 1977, the difference between male and female participation in full-time education (for all 16-year-olds) was only 5% (Central Bureau of Statistics 1979: 50). At the college level, very significant male-female differences still persist: In 1977, only 27.4% of the Dutch college student population was female.

REFERENCES

ADLER, F. (1975) Sisters in Crime. New York: McGraw-Hill.

BERENDS, A. B. and A. C. BOELMANS-KLEINJAN (1979) Beroepsarbeid door Vrouwen in Nederland. 's-Gravenhage: Staatsuitgeverij.

BLOCK, R. (1982) "Patterns of homicide across time and culture: A study of Amsterdam and Chicago." (unpublished)

Centraal Bureau voor de Statistiek [Central Bureau of Statistics] (1979) 1899-1979 Tachtig Jaren Statistiek in Tijdreeksen. 's-Gravenhage: Staatsuitgeverij.

——— (1970) Bevolking van Nederland naar Geslacht, Leeftijd en Burgerlijke Staat 1830-1969. 's-Gravenhage: Staatsuitgeverij.

——— (1966-1978) Maandstatistiek Politie en Justitie (May). 's-Gravenhage: Staatsuitgeverij.

——— (1960-1977) Criminele Statistiek. 's-Gravenhage: Staatsuitgeverij.

——— (1957-1965) Maandstatistiek van Rechtswezen, Politie en Branden (May). 's-Gravenhage: Staatsuitgeverij.

——— (1952-1955) Criminele Politele Statistiek (December) s'-Gravenhage: Staatsuitgeverij.

KOOY, G. A. (1979a) "Variatie in emancipatiebehoeftigheid anno 1978." Wageningen. (unpublished)

——— (1979b) "De Nederlandse vrouw anno 1978." Bevolking en Gezin 1 (April): 85-98.

MEYER, J. L. (1977) Sociale Atlas van de Vrouw 's-Gravenhage: Staatsuitgeverij.

SIMON, R. J. (1975) Women and Crime. Lexington, MA: D. C. Heath.

STEFFENSMEIER, D. J. (1980) "Sex differences in patterns of adult crime, 1965-77: a review and assessment." Social Forces 58: 1081-1108.

——— (1978) "Crime and the contemporary woman: an analysis of changing levels of female property crime, 1960-75." Social Forces 57: 566-584.

WEEDA, C. J. [ed.] (1981) Vrouw en Samenleving. Assen, Holland: Van Gorcum.

7

Knowlton Johnson
University of Alaska, Anchorage

LAW ENFORCEMENT SELECTION PRACTICES
The United States and Canada

Intelligent use of police authority depends ultimately on the qualifications of individuals who deal directly with the diverse populations of progressively urbanized societies and the array of events that comprises law enforcement work. The management tools for raising the quality of manpower are recruitment and training. This chapter is concerned with selection practices in recruitment that increasingly have been recognized. Those practices have been insufficiently defined and recently have become controversial in the United States because of adverse impact on the recruitment of women and members of minority groups (Lock, 1979). The unresolved role of the police in contemporary democratic societies has contributed to the controversy (Radalet, 1980) as well as to the international dimensions to be considered.

Two controversial personnel selection issues need to be addressed by international law enforcement. One issue is the general underlying philosophy of the selection practices; the other is the implementation practices of particular selection methods. In regard to police selection philosophy, it appears that the controversy centers on whether law enforcement agencies endorse a negative or positive selection approach (Territo, 1977; Stinchcomb, 1979). Negative selection emphasizes weeding out unqualified or undesirable applicants from the system. This screen-

AUTHOR'S NOTE: I wish to thank Chloe Clark-Berry, research analyst, and Chet Cottongin, Public Safety Personnel Director, for their valuable assistance in data collection and interpretation stages of the research. Appreciation is also extended to the Alaska Department of Public Safety and the Justice Center, University of Alaska, Anchorage for providing funds for this research.

out approach may be viewed as indicative of the use of a multiple or successive hurdle scoring method (Cascio and Real, 1979). The multiple hurdle scoring usually means rejection from the process if the applicant fails a particular stage.

Positive selection implies screening into the system those individuals who possess the special qualifications to perform the police role effectively. This screen-in approach is associated with a composite scoring method. Scoring in this manner permits the applicant to complete each stage or stages, and all data about an applicant are considered in the total score for all stages of the selection process, then the use of a composite score method reflects a positive selection philosophy. If the composite score method is used only for those applicants who successfully exceed a designated cutoff in one or more stages, then the use of this method characterizes a modified negative selection philosophy.

Opponents of the negative approach contend that a screening-out philosophy, while eliminating certain candidates, does not always eliminate those who are unqualified. This philosophy may also justify the use of methods that unnecessarily and unfairly eliminate those applicants who are or could become qualified through training (McCreedy, 1974). Adversaries of the positive selection usually argue that screening in is not practical with the large number of applicants most departments have to process.

Application of selection methods has also been controversial. The written test has dominated this debate (Katz, 1978; Eisenberg and Murray, 1974). A written exam is used to determine an applicant's cognitive abilities while intelligence tests are used to assess the cognitive potential of applicants. The major criticisms have been that test scores do not correlate with job performance and that minorities score lower because of the cultural bias of written exams and intelligence tests. Questions have been raised about the job-relatedness of cognitive indicators and the validation of tests (Schacter, 1979; Rosenfeld and Thornton, 1976).

Methods for collecting psychological and behavioral data have also been in the spotlight. Particular attention has been given to the lack of predictability and cultural bias of personality tests like the MMPI (Gettinger, 1981). Additionally, there has been much discussion about the role psychologists should play in police selection (Crosby, 1979; Sheahy and Roberts, 1980) and the value of situational tests as a psychological screening device (Mills, 1976).

Testing physical agility is still another area that has been in contention in recent years (Evans, 1980). Questions about the use of physical agility as a selection criterion has come under fire primarily because of the increasing number of women who aspire to become law enforcement officers. More recently, controversy has been generated by selection devices used in conjunction with an assessment center approach (Dunnette and Motowidlo, 1975; Ross, 1980) and academy and field training (Angell and Gilson, 1972; Bosarge, 1981a). The major questions being raised concern cost and practicality.

The oral board and the background investigation interview appear to be the least controversial ways of collecting data on applicants' attitudes and past behavior, even though neither of these methods have been proven to yield data that predicts future job performance (Territo, et al, 1977; Wollack, 1977). However, the use of the polygraph as a background investigation device has raised some ethical concerns.

The controversy concerning the selection philosophy and selection practices of law enforcement agencies provides the impetus for the present study. The inquiry had international dimensions because departments of the United States and Canada were surveyed. As comparative research, the study represents a useful preliminary examination of an insufficiently explored aspect of international law enforcement.

METHODS AND PROCEDURES

The study was part of a larger research project conducted by the Justice Center of the University of Alaska, Anchorage for the Alaska Department of Public Safety (Johnson and Clark, 1981). A mailed questionnaire and a telephone interview were used to collect data about police personnel practices in the United States and other countries with policing situations similar to Alaska.

The focus of the mail survey was twofold: to identify those departments that had redesigned their selection process within the last 10 years to accommodate female and/or minority applicants; and to identify those departments that had participated in a personnel selection research study. The survey emphasized the following areas: written test, substitutes for the written test, oral interviews, selecting trainable candidates as opposed to qualified candidates, minorities and females, and selection systems for departments of public safety if different from police departments.

Purposive and snowball sampling techniques were used. The design for the mailed questionnaires sent to American and Canadian agencies entailed selecting a study group from three sources. In the United States we relied on the Police Executive Research Forum (PERF) 60-agency membership and the 49 state police agencies. In Canada, departments were selected if listed as members of the International Association of

Chiefs of Police. In both countries, agency representatives and noted police selection experts were asked for any jurisdictions in their vicinity that were addressing any of the issues raised in the survey. The response rate of these target populations were 60 of 60 for the PERT membership; 36 of 49 for the state police and 35 of 73 Canadian departments.

Telephone contact was made with those departments that had made extensive changes in their selection system within the last ten years, or had participated in a police selection research study. The interview, which averaged 20-30 minutes in length, was constructed to elicit detailed information about selection practices, changes that had occurred and reasons for implementing changes.

Four trained interviewers conducted telephone interviews with representatives of 85 American departments and 5 Canadian departments that had made significant changes in the past 10 years.[1] In many instances, the person interviewed was the same person who responded to the mail questionnaire. In other cases, the interview was conducted with a department psychologist, recruiter, personnel officer, or with civil service personnel.

The comparative results reported on police personnel practices in the United States and Canada pertained to data collected in 85 U.S. agencies that participated in the mail survey and telephone interview and 35 Canadian departments that returned the mail questionnaire. These results depict the type of selection philosophy underlying police selection in both countries. Further, there are comparisons in regard to the extent of use of particular selection methods within a traditional selection system. Nontraditional selection systems that were found in both countries are also discussed. Finally, descriptive information for the 85 USA departments is presented on changes in selection practices, challenges that have occurred and the initiation of validation studies. Comparative results on changes and challenges in the 35 Canadian departments are not discussed, since only a few departments had reported in the mail survey that significant changes had taken place in police selection practices.

STATE OF THE ART
IN POLICE SELECTION

Law enforcement in the United States is composed of autonomous functioning agencies that operate at the federal, state, county, and municipality levels of governments. In the United States, there is no national police force to respond to the myriad of social problems.

Therefore, general law enforcement functions are assumed by the states, counties, and municipalities. Selection practices in these general law enforcement agencies were the focus of our study in the United States.

In Canada the Royal Canadian Mounted Police, a national body, provides general public safety services to small towns and rural areas for 8 of the 10 provinces. Ontario and Quebec have their own provincial police forces, and most major cities and numerous small towns have separate municipal forces. The Canadian departments that responded to our survey included the Royal Mounted Police, provincial forces, and many of the larger municipalities of each province.

Personnel Selection Philosophy

We examined the general selection philosophy by collecting data on methods of scoring applicants. The most common method of scoring applicants was a multiple or successive hurdle method, which means rejecton from the process if the applicant fails a particular stage. We found that 78% of the U.S. departments and 53% of the Canadian departments do not allow applicants to fail any stage of the selection process and still be considered for employment. The remaining departments in both countries indicated being more flexible by allowing an applicant to fail at least one stage and still be considered for employment or to repeat a particular stage if he or she failed. Additionally, a few U.S. departments stated that after passing a qualifying stage (e.g., a written exam) applicants received points based on data from two to three selection stages, but usually only after the score for each stage exceeded a designated cutoff.

Preference points or bonus points were given in departments of both countries to applicants having desirable qualities, experiences, or skills that are designated by the department (e.g., college degree) or are required by law (e.g., veteran points). Most U.S. departments in which preference points were awarded did so in the initial selection stage; in a few departments, an applicant was allowed to bypass certain stages if he or she had a college degree or prior police experience or had been through a departmental cadet program. In Canada, we found preference points awarded for such qualities as height, age, and education, but, unlike U.S. departments, bonus points were part of an elaborate point system that had been implemented by the national and provincial departments. This system constituted a composite scoring method, but it was considered only after applicants had passed an initial weeding-out stage.

The most unique way of screening applicants was in connection with a recent move in Washington D.C.[2] After a written exam is taken, which has been approved by the U.S. Supreme Court, applicants are randomly chosen from the pool of applicants who passed the written test. This method of making final selection decisions is being seriously questioned, partly because of the arbitrary cutoff passing score on the written test.

These results that describe ways in which applicants are scored suggest that negative selection is still the dominant philosophy underlying personnel selection in law enforcement in the United States and Canada. There is evidence in both countries that departments do use bonus points or composite scoring after an initial pass-fail stage, but in all departments surveyed some type of screening-out selection practice was evident.

Police Selection Within a Traditional System

The personnel selection process in law enforcement is defined in the United States and Canada by a number of stages that begin after recruitment and preselection (i.e., evaluation of minimum requirements) activities have been completed. We found that the selection system configuration of 95% of the 85 U.S. and 35 Canadian departments was composed of 5-8 stages. Six departments reported having only three stages and two departments indicated having 10 stages. Within each stage, one or more selection methods or devices is used to collect information about applicants. The five most common selection stages included the written test, oral interview, psychological screening, physical agility test, and background investigation.

In the written testing stage of the typical law enforcement selection process, we found applicants being tested on cognitive abilities like vocabulary, math, reading comprehension, abstract reasoning, and situational reasoning. Another testing approach relies on standardized intelligence tests that are designed to measure an applicant's cognitive potential. The written testing stage was found in most U.S. law enforcement departments (93%) and in a majority of Canadian departments (89%). It was commonly the first stage in U.S. departments (78%); however, in Canada, only 49% of the departments reported it as the first stage in the selection process.

Among the departments surveyed, the oral interview ranked second only to the written test in the United States as one of the most commonly used techniques (88%), and ranked first in Canada as the most frequently used selection method (100%). While Canada and the United States relied heavily on the oral interview, these countries sequenced this stage differently. Over half of the Canadian departments surveyed (57%) introduced applicants to the oral testing stage at either the first or second stage in the process. In the United States, 95% of the departments placed this stage at or near the end of the process. Another noticeable difference between the application of the oral interview in these two countries was that in Canada we found some departments using a one-person interview in the initial screening stage, whereas in the United States the oral interview was predominantly conducted by a board at the end of the process. In most U.S. and Canadian departments, there was only a single oral interviewing stage; however, in 14% of the U.S. and 17% of the Canadian departments surveyed, two or three oral interviews were conducted at different stages of the selection process.

The purpose of establishing a psychological screening stage has been to identify those persons who are unfit for police work as well as identifying those who have a personality appropriate for the demands and rigors of a law enforcement career. Of the U.S. departments, 51% and 57% of the Canadian departments surveyed confirmed use of some method of psychological screening. A breakdown of screening methods used to determine psychological fitness by their popularity among the American departments surveyed is as follows: 33% of the departments use only psychological tests; 5% of the departments require an interview by a psychologist; 8% of the departments combine psychological testing with an interview by a psychologist; 5% require state certification involving psychological testing and an interview by a psychologist.

Although the majority of U.S. and Canadian departments with a psychological screening component use psychological tests which are a pencil-and-paper type, the tests themselves differ in makeup, purpose, and method. Among the different types are intelligence, interest and preference, personality, and social maturity. As reflected in the literature and survey results, the Minnesota Multiphasic Personality Inventory (MMPI) continues to be the most popular standardized test, even though it is considered suspect by some psychologists. Conversely, a less widely used test, the California Psychological Inventory (CPI) has been referred to as the "sane man's MMPI" and some psychologists believe it may provide a more useful personality assessment device for use in research on police selection.

The final two traditional stages that were examined in this study were physical agility testing (PAT) and the background investigation (BI) stages of the selection process. With respect to the PAT, its basic purpose has been to weed out those candiates who, due to physiological impediments or lack of coordination, for example, will not be able to withstand the physical stress of police work. Typical events of the physical agility test include exercises in speed, endurance, agility, and strength.

Of the U.S. departments interviewed, 78% indicated that this stage was incorporated into the selection process, while 51% of the Canadian departments surveys reported that the PAT was being used. Several additional Canadian departments indicated that an agility test was being considered.

The background investigation, which 95% of all U.S. and 100% of the Canadian departments report using, also serves to weed out undesirables. The common areas in which the investigator focuses are work history, employment record, military record, educational background, criminal record, family-marital history, financial stability-credit, medical history, and the use of narcotics or alcohol. The most noticeable difference between U.S. and Canada selection practice concerned the use of the polygraph in the background investigation. We found this investigative device being used by 41% of the 85 U.S. departments surveyed but only 8% of the 35 Canadian departments. Two U.S. departments and one Canadian department indicated only using the polygraph in unusual circumstances where further determination of a candidate's credentials was necessary (i.e., used only to check the accuracy of information obtained by other selection methods.)

Selection Practices Within Alternative Systems

We uncovered three unique selection system configurations that were atypical in the United States or Canada, but conceivably are viable considerations for planning for change. These were selection systems that included an assessment center approach, observation in the academy and in a field training program, and a demonstration school.

The assessment center approach has been said to be one of the more innovative selection practices that has been introduced in law enforcement in the last 10 years. Assessment centers have been used most widely in the private sector, and only in the last 15 years have they been incorporated into the law enforcement field, most noticeably in regard to promotion. Its use for selecting entry-level officers has been gaining popularity in the last few years, but the expense of implementing the method has deterred widespread use.

The approach emphasizes a multiple assessment technique in which multiple evaluators assess a group of individuals using a variety of situational tests and simulated exercises. Attention is placed on behavior in connection with crime prevention, report writing, dispute resolution, interaction with the community, and team policing, among others. The true assessment center can replace the written exam, psychological screening, and oral interview stages of the selection process.

In our survey, we found 8 U.S. and 2 Canadian departments using the assessment center approach as a separate stage of the selection process, usually as a final stage prior to the academy. Unfortunately, the high cost of administering the assessment center has resulted in its being dropped by some departments—for example, Ft. Collins, Colorado, one of the earliest departments to use the method. One effort to minimize cost has been to set up regional assessment centers where a number of departments can send final applicants for testing prior to selection in the academy. This is being done in British Columbia, Canada[3] as well as Florida,[4] reportedly with good results.

Another emerging feature in personnel selection for law enforcement is to use academy training and/or field training programs as an observatory which constitutes the final stages of the selection process. In these final stages, the applicant's behavior (i.e., job performance) is observed and evaluated in the academy training and on-the-job training settings. If a candidate successfully completes these stages, he or she becomes a commissioned law enforcement officer.

During the early 1970s, the Dayton Police Department considered academy training one of the most critical stages of the selection process. Additionally, the San Jose Police Department has considered field training and, further, has validated the field training. Recently, Florida has incorporated the "systematic approach" for hiring, by integrating all phases of hiring, training, and retention of officers into a six-part process, including recruitment, recruit selection, psychological testing, classroom academy training, field training officer program, and probation.

A third unique selection system configuration included a "demonstration school."[5] When this school is added to the selection process, applicants who have completed all selection stages successfully (prior to the academy) spend one week attending a school designed to present a realistic view of police work. Candidates are given an opportunity to raise questions about law enforcement careers, discuss the benefits and pitfalls of a law enforcement career and interact with sworn officers. Additionally, candidates must complete physical tests and other coursework. By the end of the week, both candidates and department have a better opportunity to assess the candidate's suitability for the job. Candidates who complete their schooling successfully then go into academy training.

Controversy and Change in
U.S. Police Selection Practices

During the past 10 years, continuing controversy and change have occurred in U.S. police selection practices. Conversely, Canadian police selection methods were reported being challenged on rare occasions.[6] Moreover, in the Canadian departments surveyed, we discovered that extensive changes had been made in preselection criteria (e.g., height and gender requirements); but with the exception of the Royal Mounted Police, the provincial departments, and several municipal forces, minimal changes have been made in selection practices. As such, only the extent and nature of the controversy and changes in U.S. selection practices are discussed below.

Written test. One of the most serious complaints from applicants, administrators, and the courts is that the written test does not measure an applicant's potential for performance in the law enforcement field (i.e., lack of predictive validity). In addition, the traditionally used tests have been found to be culturally biased against minority group members and lacking in job-relatedness. Our survey highlighted this pattern of concern in that, of the 47 U.S. departments (55%) whose selection process had been challenged, 26 were because of complaints against the written test.

Efforts to rectify past deficiencies have resulted in a variety of changes being made in the written test by police and civil service departments in the last 10 years. Of the U.S. departments surveyed, 89% noted having made at least one change in the written test stage of the selection process, the following being most often mentioned: modification of current test content, modification of scoring method, development or substitution of new test, and deletion of test or substitution of alternative method. Notably, 58% of the departments that indicated having made changes in the written testing stage did so because of being challenged or the potential for being challenged.

The kind of changes being made in the written testing stage has been to make the tests more job-related, usually through an expensive validation process. We found that 58% of the U.S. departments reported having the written test validated, which was often conducted by an outside consulting firm or university.[7]

Efforts have also been made to develop written tests in the United States that can be transported and administered in multiple jurisdictions. For example, the Educational Testing Service (ETS), in conjunction with the International Association of Chiefs of Police (IACP) and International Personnel Management Association (IPMA), has developed a multijurisdictional examination for entry-level police officers

(Rosenfeld and Thornton, 1976). Although the U.S. survey results did not discover any particular test being widely used among departments in different jurisdictions, we did note that within certain states (e.g., Texas and California) the same examination is administered to different department's applicants for entry-level police work.

A few U.S. departments (7 of the 85 surveyed) either have gone so far as to eliminate the traditioinal, cognitive-based written test or have found options to this selection device. The particular options noted are use of a written test based on life experience and self-analysis, use of a background history questionnaire filled out with application form, waiver of the written test for applicants with a college degree or prior police experience, and use of the oral interview, psychological tests, and assessment center approach in place of the written test.

Oral interview. There has also been a considerable amount of change noted in the oral interviewing stage of the U.S. departments during the last 10 years. Of the departments, 44% indicated having made changes in the content of the interview and 70% noted changes in interview procedures and structure of the board. In regard to interview content, change was reported in the type of questions asked and the atmosphere in which they were being asked. We found in the survey that U.S. departments are asking more structured questions that are job-related and quantifiable, and are creating an atmosphere that allows the applicant an opportunity to provide full explanations. There was also evidence that some departments were beginning to introduce situational testing (i.e., simulated exercises) at the oral interviewing stage. This new feature provides oral board members with behavior data on applicants.

We also found that departments were beginning to emphasize a relaxed atmosphere for applicants during the interview as opposed to a stressful situation. Techniques being used that might achieve this purpose include bilingual oral exams, altering the seating arrangement of board members, use of minority-female board members especially when interviewing minority-female applicants, and preoral orientation before going into the interview.

As indicated above, 60 (70%) of the U.S. departments surveyed have made recent changes in the structure and/or procedure of the oral interview. The survey reflected that the composition of the oral boards is becoming more diverse. In addition to using civil service and departmental personnel on selection boards, departments are including community representatives, minority and female officers, and psychologists. Preparation for board members has also increased. Of the U.S. departments, 50 reported having some type of preparation (i.e. oral, written, and/or workshops) for the oral board members. Those departments that emphasized some type of preparation for board members also stressed consistency in scoring applicants. Of particular interest is that in several departments, validation studies have emphasized interscorer reliability among board members.

While there have been changes made in the oral interviewing stage of most U.S. departments surveyed, only 8 departments reported challenges in this stage of the selection process. All of these challenges were settled out of court. In regard to validation studies, the survey indicated that only 14% of the departments had validated their oral interview; all did so in connection with validation of the entire selection process.

Psychological screening. The most significant change reported in psychological screening was that departments reported relying more on psychologists and situation testing (applicable to individuals and groups). The psychologist has become more involved in the selection process in recent years, possibly because of the more widespread acceptance of psychologists in law enforcement. Among the survey departments in the United States, we found that 40% employed psychologists and 77% indicated that they do utilize outside psychologists on occasion. One state (Texas) indicated requiring certification of the psychological fitness of law enforcement candidates.

The situational testing method, which is based on simulated exercises, produces job-related behavioral data, particularly behavioral information in regard to interpersonal skills. In several instances, we found among the departments surveyed that situational testing was associated with the oral interviewing stage, and in several other cases, the method was introduced as part of an established psychological screening stage. Even though the tests seem to be more closely aligned to actual job performance, the expense seems to deter widespread use.

In terms of litigation and validation studies in connection with psychological screening methods, there has been little activity during the past 10 years in either of these areas. Of the U.S. survey departments, only 6 reported that their psychological screening methods and procedures had been challenged. Similarly, we were only able to find 4 departments that had validated the psychological screening devices. Usually these methods were validated as a part of a larger validation of the entire selection process.

Physical agility and the background investigation. Among U.S. departments, 65% indicated that changes had been made in physical agility tests during the last 10 years. A noticeable trend has been toward restructuring these tests to be more job-related by having candidates perform functions normally associated with police work. Less emphasis is being placed on the traditional push-up, pull-up, and broad jump exercises. Much of this change has been stimulated by the high litigation potential stemming from the fact that in 14 of the 47 departments reporting challenges in the selection process, all have been in connection with the PAT. As such, departments have begun to take steps not only to modify the test structure, but to help prepare applicants for the test. Some departments noted that preparation for the test is given through the use of booklets describing the test and related exercises or through physical conditioning programs to prepare applicants for the test. Also, 19 of the 85 U.S. departments indicated that a validation study had been conducted, mostly because of litigation or the litigation potential of this method.

In regard to change, in the background investigation practices in the United States, 53% of the departments surveyed indicated having made at least one change in the structure or content of the background investigation during the past 10 years (e.g., using better trained investigators or a more in-depth investigation format). The major reason given for making changes in content was that changing social norms were responsible for deleting outdated questions, or relaxing past standards (e.g., an applicant's experimentation with marijuana is not necessarily an automatic reason for rejection). Question content has also been changed in part due to increased privacy laws and guidelines that prohibit certain types of questions.

The BI stage of U.S. departments has seldom been challenged—only 6 of the 47 challenged departments in the U.S. survey. When contested, this stage has come under fire from applicants and the courts for being discriminatory in its content, or for having an adverse impact on members of minority groups. Validation action was found to be limited to only 5 (6%) of the 85 U.S. departments. This may be due to the difficulty associated with the assessment of this facet of the process.

SUMMARY AND CONCLUSIONS

Selection practices in law enforcement have been said to be one of the most complex facets of personnel management. In an effort to document the stage of this complexity internationally, the study presented provides state of the art information about police personnel practices in the United States and Canada.

The results have shown that similarities and differences do exist in the selection practices of these two countries. In regard to police personnel philosophy, the departments surveyed in United States and Canada reflect a strong negative selection orientation with all departments reporting to some degree using a pass-fail scoring method. Canada, more so than the United States, adheres to positive selection by incorporating a composite scoring method after an initial pass-fail stage.

The United States and Canada are similar regarding the employment of the traditional selection system consisting of a written exam, psychological screening methods, oral interview, background investigation, and physical agility testing. However, these two countries are dissimilar in the sequencing of the selection stages and in the use of the polygraph. That is, many Canadian departments rely heavily on an oral interview in the initial stages in the selection process, whereas most U.S. departments favor the written exam as the initial screening stage. In addition, few departments in Canada use the polygraph, while almost half of the United States departments use this device.

Both countries have piloted alternative selection systems that incorporate the assessment center approach. The concept of regionalized centers is growing. In the United States there is a push to use observation at the academy and field training stage as a regular selection method and to formalize training as stages of the selection system. Another unique stage that has been piloted in the United States is a demonstration school where final candidates and sworn officers mingle in a relaxed atmosphere.

The results showed that there has been continued controversy surrounding police selection practices in the United States. Also, U.S. departments have engaged in extensive changes in an effort to bring the selection criteria more closely in focus with actual job responsibilities; however, much of the impetus has come from outside departmental walls and has centered on reassessment and modification of current selection methods.

More controversy and, hence, research has been conducted with respect to the written test than any other method. In the United States it has consistently come under fire for lack of validity (in testing what it is supposed to), but remains in use by nearly all departments (supplemented by validation studies to prove its job-relatedness). The oral interview remains a method cemented into the process, and changes in the oral board makeup and interview content reflect efforts to make the interview a more accurate method of measuring a person's interpersonal skills. In the area of psychological screening, comparatively little has changed, in that most departments administer a standardized test. However, there appears to be a trend toward more use of psychologists in the selection process. In both the oral interview and psychological screening stages, some departments are incorporating use of situational tests and simulation exercises to observe an applicant's behavior in real life situations.

The physical agility tests are being redesigned to shift focus from exercises of strength to physical exercises more representative of actual police duties. Candidates are also given better preparation to complete this test successfully. Much of the change noted with respect to the background interview has been to streamline the interview to exclude discriminatory or irrelevant questions and to focus more in-depth on the applicant's background characteristics such as criminal record, and so on.

What new directions can be offered for the 1980s that pertain to personnel selection in international law enforcement? These study results suggest, at least in the United States, that there has been extensive change pertaining to police personnel practices; however, the parameters of these changes are set by a negative selection philosophy all departments surveyed in the U.S. and Canada endorse to some degree. We can decide to reconceptualize police selection as a process by which applicants would be screened in entirely on the basis of positive attributes and/or their potential ability to be trained to perform law enforcement tasks.[8]

The idea would be to view the process as beginning with no candidates available for x number of unfilled positions for which y acceptable candidates have to be found. This is in contrast to the traditional view, which sees the process beginning with a large pool of applicants, most of which have to be screened out. Additionally, a screen-in approach directs the use of selection devices to search for positive information about applicants' trainability rather than negative information assumed to affect applicants' ability to perform law enforcement tasks. Also, a truly positive selection system creates reinforcements at each stage of the process to ensure that applicants have the opportunity to demonstrate their maximum potential. Conversely, a screen-out system creates hurdles that are designed to identify weakness. Finally, a positive selection system has composite scoring procedures in which applicants accumulate points for positive strengths and, unlike the screen-out system, does not screen out applicants for weaknesses not known to affect job performance negatively.

If selection criteria relates primarily to positive qualities and the trainability of applicants, this alternative selection philosophy would produce an array of changes in selection practice. The appropriateness of some methods, like written exams, intelligence tests, and personality tests, would continue to be questioned seriously. Other methods like the background investigation and oral interview could be revised to produce data about applicants' positive qualities and trainability. Also, a positive approach to selection would legitimize the assessment center approach and observation at the academy and field training stages. Finally, emphasizing positive qualities and the trainability of applicants may spark new approaches to selecting candidates for the law enforcement profession. In total, a selection philosophy as described has the potential for producing not only changes in police selection devices but also changes in other areas of personnel management, training, and ultimately, the quality of international law enforcement.

NOTES

1. Instrument construction entailed numerous work sessions with the interviewers, who participated in question construction and role-playing exercises. Additionally, pretests were conducted using three Alaskan departments: the Anchorage Police Department, the Kenai Police Department, and the Soldotna Police Department.

2. See Bosarge (1981b) for a discussion of this new initiative in police selection.

3. Twelve municipal departments in British Columbia send final candidates to the Justice Institute of British Columbia in Vancouver for one-day assessment center exercises in six areas.

4. The Miami-Dade County Assessment Center is located at Miami-Dade County Community College in Miami, Florida.

5. See McCutcheon (1977) for a discussion of this method.

6. We found, through the five telephone interviews with Canadian departments, that it was unusual for litigation to be brought against selection methods being used in law enforcement.

7. These validation studies focused on content, construct, and concurrent validity checks. Of the validation studies we were able to retrieve, none addresses the issue of predictive validity. It is worth noting that while test validation activity was not uncommon, there was no report of a systematic follow-up evaluation of changes being made in the written testing stage.

8. Credit is given posthumously to Walt Lawson, former Director of Administrative Services, Alaska Department of Public Safety for introducing the concept of trainability as a potential police selection criterion in Alaska.

REFERENCES

ANGELL, J. E. and J. GILSON (1972) "Dayton police training." Journal of Law Enforcement Education and Training 1, 2: 58.

BOSARGE, B. (1981a) "Conference explores methods for developing systematic selection training systems." Training Aids Digest 6, 6: 1.

——— (1981b) "D.C. police lower standards, choose recruits by lottery." Training Aids Digest 6, 9: 1.

CASCIO, W. F. and L. J. REAL (1979) "The civil service exam has been passed: now what?" in C. Speilberger (ed.) Police Selection and Evaluation: Issues and Techniques. Washington, DC: Hemisphere.

CROSBY, A. (1979) "The psychological examination in police selection." Journal of Police Science and Administration 7, 2: 215-229.

DUNNETTE, M. D. and S. J. MOTOWIDLO (1975) Development of a Personnel Selection and Career Assessment System for Police Officers in Patrol, Investigative, Supervisory and Command Positions. For the U.S. Dept. of Justice, LEAA, National Institute of Law Enforcement and Criminal Justice. Washington, DC: Personnel Decisions.

EISENBERG, T. and J. MURRAY (1974) "Selection," in A. O. Stahl (ed.) Police Personnel Administration. Police Foundation.

EVANS, D. H. (1980) "Height, weight and physical agility requirements: Title VII and public safety employment." Journal of Police Science and Administration 8, 4: 414-436.

GETTINGER, S. (1981) "Psychological testing of recruits can: A) screen out the real turkeys; B) spot the supercops; C) both of the above; D) neither of the above." Police Magazine (March): 30-42.

JOHNSON, K. W. and C. CLARK-BERRY (1981) Examination of Qualifying Criteria for Selection of Law Enforcement Personnel in Alaska: Final Report. Anchorage: Justice Center, University of Alaska.

KATZ, H. A. (1978) "Minimum reading and writing proficiency standards for police applicants." The Police Chief 45, 10: 297-299.

LOCKE, H. G. (1979) The Impact of Affirmative Action and Civil Service on American Police Personnel Systems. For the U.S. Department of Justice, LEAA, National Institute of Law Enforcement and Criminal Justice. Washington, DC: Government Printing Office.

McCREEDY, K. R. (1974) "Selection practices and the police role." The Police Chief 41, 7: 41.

McCUTCHEON, W. W. (1977) "St. Paul's demo school for police candidates." The Police Chief (March):46-47.

McGHEE, A. and M. E. DEEN (1979) "Utilizing the assessment center to select police officers for Ocala, Florida Department. The Police Chief 46, 8: 69-74.

MILLS, R. B. "Simulated stress in police recruit selection." Journal of Police Science and Administration 4, 2: 1979-1986.

RADELET, L. A. The Police and the Community. Encino, CA: Glenco.

ROSENFELD, M. and R. F. THORNTON (1976) The Development and Validation of a Multijurisdictional Police Examination. Chicago: International Personnel Management Assoc.

ROSS, J. D. (1980) "Determination of the predictive validity of the assessment center approach to selecting police managers." Journal of Criminal Justice 8: 89-96.

SCHACTER, H. L. (1979) "Job-related examinations for police: two developments." Journal of Police Science and Administration, 7, 1: 86-89.

SHEALY, A. E. and E. ROBERTS (1980) "Police selection," pp. 373-386 in G. Cooke (ed.) The Role of the Forensic Psychologist. Springfield, IL: Charles C Thomas.

STINCHCOMB, J. D. (1979) "Law enforcement personnel development," in D. O. Schultz (ed.) Modern Police Administration. Houston, TX: Gulf.

TERRITO, L., C. R. SWANSON, and N. C. CHAMELIN (1977) The Police Personnel Selection Process. Indianapolis: Bobs-Merrill.

Wollack and Associates (1977) Background Investigator's Manual: A Guide to the Evaluation of Municipal Police Officer Applicants. Prepared for the Texas Commission on Law Enforcement, Officers Standards and Education. Greenwood, CA: Author.

Nancy Travis Wolfe
University of South Carolina

8

PARTICIPATION IN COURTS
American Jurors and German Lay Judges

Although the right to trial by one's peers has been a fundamental principle of American jurisprudence, the petit jury is coming under increasingly sharp attack. [1] Critics frequently point to the evident unwillingness of Americans to serve as jurors and question whether this reluctance precludes the fulfillment of the constitutional guarantee to trial by an impartial jury. Since research studies indicate that many persons try to avoid jury duty because of the amount of time involved, it can be useful to compare the laws and policies of American jurisdictions with those of another method of lay participation: the mixed tribunals of the Federal Republic of Germany. The following analysis will focus on the temporal aspects of service by American petit jurors and German lay judges.

In Germany, persons are chosen from the community to serve on the bench with professional judges; in this capacity they have full powers of interrogation, deliberation, voting, and sentencing. [2] Comparison of the role of these lay judges and that of petit jurors in the United States is complicated by the basic differences in the legal framework of the two countries. [3] Unlike the dual legal system of the United States, the judicial system of Germany is unitary; state courts implement federal law as well as state law, and they are governed by federal procedural policies. Significantly, in Germany there are no federal courts in which lay persons hear criminal trials; nor is there an analogue to the American

AUTHOR'S NOTE: I wish to express appreciation for financial aid provided by the American Philosophical Society and the German Academic Exchange Service, which facilitated this research.

grand jury. Despite the differences in legal structures, examination of temporal patterns of service of lay judges may suggest modifications that could be considered in American courts.[4]

In the criminal courts of the Federal Republic, lay judges serve in four types of tribunals.[5] German lay judges (*Laienrichter*) are designated by different labels, according to the court in which they appear. In criminal cases they are called *Schöffen,*[6] whereas in the other types of courts (civil, administrative, finance, labor and social courts) they are referred to as *ehrenamtliche Richter.* A person being charged with a criminal offense[7] will be tried either in a court that consists of both professional and lay judges, or, if he is tried for a petty crime by a professional judge sitting alone, he has a right to a second hearing before such a court. In the court of limited jurisdiction, the *Amtsgericht,* there is a mixed tribunal called a *Schöffengericht.* Under certain circumstances the composition of the mixed tribunal of the Amtsgericht may be expanded through the addition of another professional judge; this *Erweitertes Schöffengericht,* therefore, consists of two professional and two lay judges.

At the second level of court, the *Landericht* (general criminal jurisdiction), there are three mixed tribunals. The *Kleine Strafkammer* (with one professional and two lay judges) is a court of second hearing for cases appealed from the Amtsgericht in instances where a single professional judge held the original trial. For the more serious crimes a *Grosse Strafkammer* (with three professional and two lay judges) has original jurisdiction, as well as review jurisdiction for cases coming from the Schöffengericht of the Amtsgericht; again the rehearing is *de novo.* As in the Amtsgericht, there is provision for a special lay judge court, called the *Schwurgericht*; this tribunal is composed of three professional and two lay judges, and it has jurisdiction over the most serious crimes, such as murder and aggravated arson.

WILLINGNESS TO SERVE

Analysts of the jury system frequently comment on attitudes of Americans toward jury service. The willingness of individuals to serve affects the representativeness of jury panels and may, therefore, affect verdicts. Legal experts and research scholars express polar views on the question of willingness. Chief Warren Burger, for instance, speaking at a conference of Chief Justices in 1979, noted that "overwhelmingly, as every trial judge and trial lawyer knows, a great many of the people best qualified to sit on juries are those most eager to escape jury duty" (Burger, 1979; 3; Stoever, 1974). A study in 1973 reported that "some citizens will do anything — including lying under oath — to avoid sitting on a jury" (U.S. News and World Report, 1973: 28). Surveys, however, indicate that persons who actually serve on juries express favorable attitudes. Pabst et al. (1976: 164) wrote, "Yet, amazingly, the majority of citizens who fail to wriggle out of jury duty look back on it as a positive experience." Richert (1977b: 497) criticized this conclusion, saying that an attempt to evaluate juror willingness should include all of the jurors who had been summoned, not just those who serve on juries.[8]

In another study, Richert (1977a: 497) spoke of the benign neglect of the question of jury willingness in empirical scholarship, despite the fact that the issue of jury representativeness has been a growing concern. Because refusal to serve can seriously affect the representativeness of juries, Richert questioned a sample of citizens who had been veniremen. He found that more than half had asked to be excused from service.

Regardless of the lack of conclusive data pertaining to the percentage of eligible Americans who resist jury service, it is evident that a significant number has a negative attitude. The crucial question, then, is to determine the reasons for this reluctance. Recently a survey was made of 3,000 jurors across the country; these jurors, representing 18 courts, indicated that the aspects most disliked about jury service were (1) long periods of time waiting in the jury room, (2) never being selected to sit on a jury, and (3) long terms of jury service (Canham, 1977: 1). The same survey found that "many citizens are unwilling to accept the personal costs and seek excuses from jury duty." Criticism of long jury service has been summarized by Canham, who found that the longer tenure negatively affects the representativeness of jury composition; citizens were tremendously inconvenienced; jurors were bored, frustrated, underutilized; and repeated use of the same juror led to "professional juror syndrome" (1977: 35-36).

Evidence of recognition of the importance of tenure in regard to juror attitude is the publication of a "Juror's Bill of Rights" in the *Newsletter of the Center for Jury Studies* (a program established under the Law Enforcement Assistance Administration, now merged with the National Center for State Courts). One of the rights included was a stipulation that the length of jury duty be sufficiently short that normal activities would not be unduly disturbed by jury service (September 1979). Another was the right to be utilized efficiently (e.g., summoned into court only when there was a strong likelihood that a juror would be needed in *voir dire* or in actual service). Some states still summon talesmen (bystanders) when an insufficient number of prospective jurors is available. A study of juror attitudes made by the National Institute of Law Enforcement and Criminal Justice supported a conclusion that willingness was "formed largely by the efficiency and orderliness with which their time has been used. A judge's actions, especially in showing appreciation for juror's time, can have a profound influence on their view of the court" (*Guide to Juror Usage,* 1974).

Length of Tenure

The required length of service is controversial in the United States and Germany. Two related issues are the frequency of service and the maximum number of years or days a layperson may serve. There is a distinct difference in the two systems: In the United States jurors are summoned for a block of time; in West Germany the *Laienrichter* are assigned to sessions over a period of four years (usually one day a month).

Most statutes of American states prescribe a maximum period of service but do not establish a minimum (Newsletter, March 1981). The average term of service of a juror is ten days (*Guide to Juror System Management,* 1975). Some jurors serve much longer, however; a publication of the National Institute of Justice indicated that 20- or 30-day service is not unusual (Dogin, 1980). States are experimenting with shorter tenure periods; for example, in Utah jurors serve only 10 days (Newsletter, March 1979). Other states are making more drastic reductions through programs requiring service for "one day or one trial" (Carlson, 1977). Jurors are summoned to appear for the venire on a certain day; if a venireman is chosen to sit on a jury, he is then obligated for the entire length of the trial. Should he not be selected during the day for which he was called to court, his obligation is then at an end. Such a juror utilization method has been in use in Wayne County, Michigan since 1975, and initial analyses suggest that it is successful (Kasunic, 1979). Another study of the one day-one trial system showed higher juror satisfaction; of those who served a one-month term, 88% indicated a favorable reaction, whereas of the jurors who served one day, 92% responded favorably (Burke, 1977).[9] The LEAA has encouraged experimentation with shorter terms through provision of grant money; courts were to incorporate 12 specific elements into their jury systems (Newsletter, March 1979). One of the elements was the one day-one trial systems "whenever practicable to lessen the burden of jury duty on individuals."

Jury selection and service in the federal courts of the United States are controlled by Title 28; Article 1864 stipulates that "from time to time," as directed by the district court, the clerk is to summon the requisite number of persons to serve on a venire. Persons summoned on venire are obligated for the term of court (usually about a month). Federal courts, like those of the states, attempt to avoid burdening veniremen unnecessarily, and in some districts "on call" systems have been implemented; jurors may remain at home or at work until notified by the jury commissioner. Veniremen chosen to hear a specific trial are obligated for the length of the trial. Unfortunately, there appears to be a trend toward longer trials in the federal courts; a 1980 report indicated an increase of 14.5% (over the previous year) for trials lasting four days or more (*Report of the Proceedings of the Judicial Conference of the United States,* 1980).

While the U.S. courts seem to be moving toward briefer tenure, German law has recently extended the period of obligation. In the Federal Republic, the length of tenure for lay judges has varied during the 130 years since the first mixed bench in modern Germany.[10] In the Hanover Model of mixed tribunal, introduced in 1850, Schöffen served one-year terms. When the traditional type of jury was abolished in 1923 and the Schöffengerichte was established, the law specified that lay judges were to be selected every two years (Gesetz [Law] 11.7.1923 RGBl. I 647). Since that time an extended service period has been suggested, as long as eight years; in revisions of the Court Organization Act being considered by the Bundesrat and the Bundestag, various rationales have been expressed for either shortening or lengthening the obligation of *Laienrichter.* A short duration is urged by those experts who would avoid overburdening lay judges (*Drucksache,* 7/2600: 10). The *Bundesregierung* held three years to be the maximum (Rüping, 1976). Although a briefer obligation might foster wider lay participation in courts, the experience of the German states under the two-year tenure law found little change in representativeness. As before, the older members of the population were overrepresented and women were underrepresented (*Drucksache,* 7/551: 54).

Proponents of longer tenure have predicted increased effectiveness of lay participation. Liekefett (1965) refers to the lack of forensic experience among lay judges and recommends a four-year period of office.

Jescheck believes increasing the tenure to four years would allow the Laienrichter to gain more experience, expert knowledge, and certainty (1977). Nowakowski (1970) failed to find evidence that lengthened terms in a part-time capacity increased legal experience and understanding of legal questions.

Advocacy of lengthened tenure is often grounded on the lower administrative expense when selection is carried out less frequently (*Drucksache,* 7/2600: 10). The administrative task also may be lightened by giving the states greater flexibility in the number of persons to be placed on the lists of potential lay judges or by a simpler method of selecting the names, perhaps according to the first letter of the names or of the streets (Löwe-Rosenberg [Schäfer], Gerichtsverfassungsgezetz [Law of Court Constitution] Article 36, Randnummer 1). Some analysts have proposed a three-year obligation, but the Bundesrat urged the adoption of a four-year tenure; this position was supported by reference to similar practices in the administrative, fiscal, and social courts (Rüping, 1976). In the Court Organization Act of 1975, the four-year term was codified (GVG, Article 36).

Sequestration is a practice in American courts for which there is no counterpart in Germany. Where the judge believes it necessary for a fair hearing, he can require that the jury be isolated during the trial. Although rare, the procedure is highly intrusive into the lives of the jurors; they are in the custody of the government 24 hours a day, subject not only to physical restrictions but also to censorship of telephone calls, mail, newspapers, and entertainment. Where there is a long process of selection of jurors for a trial, each juror must remain sequestered from the moment he is chosen for service.

Number of Persons Called for Service

Overcall results in alienation of jurors and unnecessary expense for the American courts, and ultimately for the public. Assembly of an appropriately sized venire is complicated by the uneven nature of the demand for jury trial. Because of uncertainty regarding the need for a jury trial (affected unpredictably, inter alia, by plea bargaining, waiver of jury trial by defendants, postponements of trial or dismissals of cases, etc.), jury commissioners have to weigh two values—the optimum allocation of resources in the courts and the minimization of the burden on jurors. One study suggests that if a judge in a court has never been caused to wait by lack of sufficient contingent of jurors, that court is calling too many jurors in on venire (Burke, 1977).

A more realistic estimate of the number of jurors required is possible with the increased accuracy and completeness of court records resulting from court unification in the states. Within a given jurisdiction, the numbers of past trials in a certain time span and their average length can be measured more precisely and future trials predicted more accurately for months, days of the week, and times of day (Guide to Juror Usage, 1974). The jury commissioner can check records to determine yield percentage through past experience on how many jurors qualified of the number summoned.

Federal jurisdictions have begun using computerized information for "juror usage indexes" as a gauge of efficiency. The index represents the average number of jurors available for each jury trial day, and it is derived by dividing the total number of available jurors by the total number of jury trial days. In 1982, the Juror Usage Index was 17.91, ranging from a low of 11.41 in Wyoming to a high of 24.04 in Puerto Rico (Statistical Analysis and Reports Division, 1982: 11).[11]

The one day-one trial approach would involve a far larger number of jurors but at the same time would decrease the amount of time spent in court by any one juror. In the federal courts, the percentage of jurors summoned on venire who are not selected, do not serve, or are not challenged has shown a downward trend (from 24.1 in 1977 to 21.9 in 1982); nevertheless, it is evident that far more jurors are summoned than utilized (Statistical Analysis and Reports Divison, 1982: 17).

In the Federal Republic of Germany the appointment of a number of lay judges can be geared more precisely to the requirements of the courts, because a defendant does not have a choice between a bench and a jury trial and because the composition of the court is constant. The date and length of the trial are more predictable in the inquisitorial system where the judge determines the nature of the proceedings (kinds of evidence needed, which witnesses to summon, etc.). A German trial need not be so long as an American one. Without a jury, the rules of evidence are simplified and there is no need to remove a jury for hearings of motions. Decisions on guilt can be reached by less than unanimous vote.

Selection of the Schöffen begins with the list of nominees drawn up by the community council (GVG, Article 36; Herrmann, 1979); as in the United States, there is a legislative mandate for representativeness.[12] Although intended to be random, the actual practice appears to be close to a "key man" method of identification of potential jurors. The German scholar Fritz Baur (1968) wrote that lay judges were "not chosen by the people and not chosen from the people." Next, the list is submitted to the local county court (GVG, Article 38; Katholnigg, 1980; Kern, 1954). A candidate for lay judge is not required to present himself during the selection process as are American veniremen, thus avoiding unnecessary interference in the lives of lay judges. A committee chooses, by two-thirds of the vote, Schöffen for the next four-year period (GVG, Article 42). Repeated service as a lay judge is not excluded, but the code specifies that persons who have been lay judges in criminal courts for eight years should not be chosen if their last year of service was less than eight years earlier (GVG, Article 34[7]).

Only the number actually required is summoned for duty as principal lay judges, called *Hauptschöffen,* or as alternates, called *Hilfsschöffen.* Presidents in the state courts (Landgerichte or Amtsgerichte) determine the requisite number according to a formula (GVG, Article 43).[13] The number is calculated on the basis of (1) the need of the courts (the expected number of session days is to be multiplied by 2 and then divided by 12 in order to yield sufficient lay judges to have two available for each session) and (2) a limit of 12 days of service for an individual Schöffee; the earlier version of the law (the Unification Act of 1950) had set 12 as a minimum; the number of Hauptschöffen is to be determined so that each is drawn for no more than 12 ordinary session days per year. Persons who have been Laienrichter previously may decline to serve if called, as may persons who, in the foregoing period of office for honorary judges, have already completed 40 days of service (GVG, Article 35 [2]; Schlotheim, 1965). Because the exact number of possible occasions requiring Hilfsschöffen cannot be predicted, there is no precise statutory instruction for the alternates (Riess, 1982; Röper, 1981). The rule is that the number of Hilfsschöffen is to be in a suitable relationship to that of Hauptschöffen in order to avoid an excessive burden on the alternates.

Assignment of Jurors and Lay Judges

Procedures for identifying jurors in the United States to hear a particular case differ from the methods of assignment of lay judges in Germany. The prospective juror is summoned by court to appear on a certain day; he then may be chosen to hear a specific case. Lay judges in Germany are selected by the community council of a district and are then assigned to a court and a day.

In courts of both state and federal jurisdiction in the United States, assignment to a trial jury involves questioning of the jurors (Federal

Rules of Criminal Procedure, Rule 24). In some jurisdictions, examination is primarily carried out by the judge; in others attorneys play a significant role. Statute law guarantees to the attorneys a right to challenge for cause if there is evidence of partiality. Usually there are specified numbers of peremptory challenges, the number being keyed to the seriousness of the offense. In Germany there is no actual counterpart of voir dire. Persons on the nomination list and the chosen lay judges can be challenged (Strafprozessordnung. [Code of Criminal Procedure], Article 31), but challenges are rare (Langbein, 1981: 208).

Each year of his tenure, a lay judge will be assigned to a specific court—either in the Schöffengericht (of the Amtsgericht) or in the Grosse Strafkammer, Kleine Strafkammer, or Schwuregericht (of the Landgericht). Werner (1974) noted that the judges assigned to the Schwuregericht would not, as a rule, know each other personally; on the other hand, they might have met through activity in the same political parties or other organizations. After being assigned, a Laienrichter can serve in only that one court. If he were to be called, during a given year, to several offices or to several courts, he is to take the office to which he was first called (GVG, Article 77 [4]). Once the names of the Hauptschöffen and Hilfsschöffen are selected, the list is divided into separate groups by the committee. One list contains names of persons for the Amtsgericht (both Hauptschöffen and Hilfsschöffen); another lists the youth court lay judges JGG, Article 35 [5]); and a third includes lay judges for the other courts.

After lay judges are assigned to a particular court, the sequence of their service is determined by a random process. The exact method is not stipulated in the law, although Article 45(2) of the GVG does require that it be done in a public session of the Amtsgericht, and the third section of the law specifies that it is the judge who is to make the random selection. One commentator describes two possible methods of assignment (Löwe-Rosenberg [Schäfer], 1979: 266). The names of all Hauptschöffen could be placed in an urn and then for each regular session two names would be drawn. Each time, the drawn names are replaced in the urn; whether the two Schöffen who have been chosen for the first (or later) sessions also serve for a subsequent sitting depends merely on chance. Another method mentioned is for each Schöffe whose name has been drawn to be assigned immediately for several sessions in a row. Because there are two Schöffen serving on a mixed tribunal, they are often assigned in pairs. The assignment is applicable for a one-year period only; so each lay judge would be reassigned in the subsequent three years of his tenure.

Following the judge's determination of sequence of service for the individual lay judges in each court, the court clerk draws up a protocol.[14] A change in the sequence of service can be made through application by the Schöffe and approval by the judge, so long as the lay judge still has not already become involved in a case. If such a change is made, the agreement must be entered into the records (GVG, Article 47).

Under the law a differentiation is made between assignment of lay judges for ordinary and extraordinary sessions. In the case of the former, the dates are established a year ahead of time. This is done under the "principle of constancy" (GVG, Article 45); it is presumed that past experience permits estimation of the required sessions for calendaring predetermined sessions days (GVG, Article 77). If the business of the court requires additional sittings, the Schöffen to be called are randomly chosen before the assigned day (GVG, Article 47).

Inasmuch as the Laienrichter are not screened in regard to particular cases, the possibility exists that in a given instance an individual Schöffe might be inappropriate for the specific hearing. Protection against partiality of judges is provided in the Criminal Code (StPO, Article 24); this stipulation applies to Laienrichter as well. Basic responsibility for the proper composition of the court lies with the presiding judge, but a Schöffe is obligated to inform him if he does not feel completely free in considering the case (Justizministerium Baden W kurttemberg, 1980). Once a lay judge begins to hear a case, he must remain on the bench until its conclusion. The length of a trial in Germany is briefer than in the United States, however. Figures for the year 1980 show that 53.3% of the criminal trials were completed in a day or less, another 21.8% within two days, and 17.7% within three to five days (Statistisches Bundesamt Wiesbaden, 1981). Should his days of service exceed 24 during a year, a Schöffe may ask to be stricken from the list of lay judges (GVG, Article 52).

Unlike the voir dire process in the United States (which involves deliberate selection for an individual trial), the later stages of the selection of lay judges apparently represent a completely random method, without attention to the suitability of a lay judge for a particular case. It is not known ahead of time how the Schof fen are to be assigned, nor are the characteristics of the lay judges made known—not even their age or gender, much less their previous experience or inclinations (Werner, 1974).

CONCLUSION

The methods of selection of American jurors and German lay judges differ sharply. In the United States, statute and case law require utilization of procedures which emphasize random selection. German law, too, specifies that lay judges are to be representative of the population; yet limited empirical research suggests that selection is a more personal procedure than in the United States. Willingness of laypersons to serve hinges on the degree to which the prospective jurors or lay judges are inconvenienced during the selection phase. Americans are often called into court for long periods of idle time, but a candidate for lay judge in Germany need not appear in court unless he wishes to apply for excusal.

At the point of assignment to hear a case, veniremen in the United States are often questioned extensively before being qualified to sit in a jury box, a process that focuses on their individual experiences and characteristics. On the contrary, German Laienrichter are assigned in a random manner, with the possibility of disqualification if partiality is indicated. Also, in sharp contrast is the amount of time consumed in American voir dires (as long as four or five months in felony cases); the assignment of lay judges in German courts as relatively simple.

Do the patterns of selection and assignment adversely affect the prospective juror or lay judge? There has been even less primary research on this point in Germany than in the United States. American studies indicate that laypersons object strongly to the time consumed by venire practices, uncertainty concerning dates and lengths of service for which they will be obligated, and the process of sequestration. It seems reasonable to conclude that the German system has an advantage in being less disruptive of the lives of its Laienrichter. Nevertheless, it is likely that the tenure of a German lay judge (who serves approximately one day per month for four years) will exceed that of an American juror (who is obligated for a term of court and/or the length of a trial). In both countries there are some restrictions on the number of times a person can be summoned for court service.

Future comparisons of service by American jurors and German *laienrichter* could include the following: practices regarding postponement and excusals, use of alternates, and length of deliberation periods. That research could offer further insights into the willingness of lay persons to participate in the judicial process.

NOTES

1. Even though 95 percent of American criminal cases are resolved without jury trial (Newsletter, November 1981), the absolute number of trials is large. In the federal courts alone, there are 35,263 trial days in 1982 (Statistical Analysis and Reports Divison, 1982). In the state jury courts, some 20 million jury days each year are devoted to 300,000 civil and criminal cases (*Guide to Jury Management,* 1975; Burger, 1981).

2. The liberal revolution of the 1840s incorporated the principle of the jury in German law. During the nineteenth century, the use of a mixed tribunal, including both lay and professional judges, reemerged, first in 1818 in Württemberg (Jescheck, 1977: 234; Justizmenesterium Schleswig-Holstein, 1976). The two forms of courts coexisted until the Emminger Reform of 1924; then the jury was abolished in Germany and, except for a brief revival in Bavaria after World War II, it has not reappeared.

3. For a comparison of the goals and functions of the United States jury and the German lay judge system, see Langbein (1981). An evaluation of the two systems is also made by Hartung (1970). Jescheck (1970, 1977) and Knittel (1970) examine the functions of mixed tribunals for felonies. Also see Herrmann (1979).

4. This chapter considers only adult criminal courts; the procedure for selection and the role of lay judges in juvenile courts differs from that of the adult courts.

5. In translations from German, the word "juror" is often used where the word "Schöffe" appears in the German text, perhaps because the lay judges do take an oath (Deutsches Richtergesezt [Law of German Judges], Article 45). To avoid confusion, the word "juror" in this chapter will refer only to courts in the United States.

6. This is an old German word which is etymologically related to the verb "to create" (*schaffen*).

7. An exception to this general rule occurs in such cases as high treason, which are heard under original jurisdiction by a five-man panel of professional judges in the *Oberlandesgericht* (Heyde, 1969).

8. Pabst et al. (1977) reply to Richert's criticisms, but the points made are not pertinent to those parts of his study that are relevant here.

9. The demographic characteristics of jurors in Bucks County, Pennsylvania, were examined after a change from two-week terms to one day-one trial tenure. Representation of white-collar persons increased from 34% in 1980 to 51% in 1981. The representation of blue-collar workers declined from 43% in 1980 to 21% in 1981 (Newsletter, July 1981).

10. For discussion of the history of lay judges, see Dahringer (1950), Brunner (1972), Mittermaier and Leipmann (1908), Jescheck (1977), Dawson (1960), and Richert (forthcoming).

11. Over the six-year period prior to 1980, the Juror Usage Index ranged between 19.12 and 19.73; in 1980, however, the figure dropped to 18.83 (Statistical Analysis and Reports Division, 1980).

12. For discussion of methods of selection, see Casper and Zeisel (1979), Klausa (1972), Langbein (1977), Richert (forthcoming), Katholnogg and Bierstedt (1982), and Schiffman (1974).

13. Earlier the state ministry of justice had carried this responsibility. See Löwe-Rosenberg (Schäfer) (1979).

14. It is then the responsibility of the judge to inform the Schöffen of their assignments and of the consequences of absence on the appointed days (GVG, Article 46).

REFERENCES

BAUR, F. (1968) "Laienrichter — heute?" Festschrift fürEduard Kern. Tübingen.

BRUNNER, H. (1872) Die Entstehung der Schwurgerichte. Berlin.

BURGER, W. E. (1981) "Is our jury system working?" Reader's Digest (February): 2-6.

BURKE, D., W. R. PABST, Jr., T. MUNSTERMAN, and M. SOLOMON (1977) Juror Usage and Management Participant's Handbook. Washington, DC: University Research Corp.

CANHAM, J. N. (1977) "One day: one trial." Judge's Journal 16: 34-51.

CARLSON, K., AL HALPER, and D. WHITCOMB (1977) An Exemplary Project: One Day/One Trial Jury System. Washington, DC: Government Printing Office.

CASPER, G. and H. ZEISEL (1979) Der Laienrichter im Strafprocess. Heidelberg: C. F. Müller.

DAHRINGER, H. (1950) "Berufs- und Laienrichter in der deutschen Rechtspflege: Geschichtliche Entwicklung seit dem Beginn des 19. Jahrhunderts." Dissertation, Albert-Ludwig-Universität, Freiburg-im-Breisgau.

DAWSON, J. P. (1960) A History of Lay Judges. Cambridge, MA: Harvard University Press.

DOGIN, H. S. (1980) Citizen's Role in the Courts. Washington, DC: Government Printing Office.

A Guide to Juror Usage (1974) Washington, DC: Government Printing Office.

A Guide to Jury System Management (1975) Washington, DC: Government Printing Office.

HARTUNG, F. (1970) "Um das Schwurgericht." Zeitschrift für die gesamte Strafrechtswissenschaft 82: 601-609.

HERRMANN, R. (1979) " Schöffen in der BRO — keine gleichberechtigten Richter." Neue Justiz, pp. 130-133.

HEYDE, W. (1969) Die Rechtspflege in der Bundesrepublik Deutschland. Oberursel/Ts: Agenor Druck- u. Verlags-GmbH.

JESCHECK, H.-H. (1977) "Laienrichtertum in der Strafrechtspflege der B undesrepublik Deutschland und der Schweiz." Schweizerische Zeitschrift für Strafrecht (Révue Pénale Suisse) 94: 229-231.

— — — (1970) "Principles of German criminal procedure in comparison with American Law." Virginia Law Review 56: 239-253.

Justizministerium Baden Württemberg (1977) Ein Leitfaden für Schöffen. Stuttgart: Author.

— — — (1976) Information für Schöffen in Schleswig-Holstein. Rendsburg: Kraft Druckerei.

KASUNIC, D. E. (1979) "One big idea for small courts." Judge's Journal 18: 44-49.

KATHOLNIGG, O. (1980) "Nochmals: Auslosung der Schöffen zur Schöffenliste des Landgerichts." Monatschrift für deutsches Recht 34: 635-636.

— — — and H. BIERSTEDT (1982) "Sind bei den Schöffen alle Gruppen der Bevölkerung angemessen berücksichtigt?" Zeitschrift für Rechtspolitik, pp. 267-269.

KERN, E. (1954) Geschichte des Gerichtsverfassungsrechts. München: C. H. Beck'sche.

KLAUSA, E. (1972) Ehrenamtliche Richter: Ihre Auswahl und Funktion, Empirisch Untersucht. Frankfurt: Athenäum.

KNITTEL, E. (1970) Mitbestimmunmg in der Strafjustiz: was soll aus dem deutschen Schwurgericht werden? Marburg: N. G. Elwert.

LANGBEIN, J. H. (1981) "Mixed court and jury court: could the continental alternative fill the American need?" American Bar Association Research Journal (Winter): 195-219.

— — — (1977) Comparative Criminal Procedure. St. Paul: West Publishing.

LIEKEFETT, K. (1965) "Die Ehrenamtlichen Richter an den Deutschen Gerichten." Dissertation, Georg-August-Universität, Göttingen.

LÖWE-ROSENBERG (1979) Die Strafprozessordnung und das Gerichtsverfassungsgesetz. Berlin: Walter de Gruyter.

MITTERMAIER, W. and M. LIEPMANN (eds.) (1980) Schwurgerichte und Schöffengerichte (2 vols.). Liepzig.

NOWAKOWSKI, F. (1970) "Reform der Laiengerichtsbarkeit in Strafsachen," in Verhandlunger des vierten ÖsterreichischenJuristentages. Wein: Manzsche Verlags- und Universitätsbuchhandlung.

PABST, W. R., Jr., G. T. MUNSTERMAN, and C. H. MOUNT (1977) "The value of jury duty: serving is believing." Judicature 61: 38-42.

――― (1976) "The myth of the unwilling juror." Judicature 60: 164-171.

Report of the Proceedings of the Judicial Conference of the United States (1980) Annual Report of the Director of the Administrative Office of the U.S. Courts.

RICHERT, J. P. (1977a) "Jurors' attitudes toward jury service." Justice System Journal pp. 233-245.

――― (1977b) "A new verdict on juror willingness." Judicature 60: 496-501.

――― (forthcoming) Citizens in the Criminal Courts: The Case of Germany.

RIESS, P. (1982) "Die Befreiung eines Schöffen von der Dienstleistung an einem bestimmten Sitzungstag kann nach Eingang bei der Schöffengeschäftsstelle nicht mehr wiederrufen werden." Juristiche Rundschau (June 6): 255-257.

RÖPER, E. (1981) "Zur Auswahl der Hilfsschöffen." Deutsche Richterzeitung 59: 99-101.

RÜPING, H. (1976) "Funktionen der Laienrichter im Strafverfahren." Juristiche Rundschau, pp. 269-274.

SCHIFFMAN, G. (1974) Die Bedeutung der ehrenamtlichen Richter bei Gerichten der allgemeinen Verwaltungsgerichtsbarkeit. Vol. 53 of Schrifterreihe der Hochschule Speyer. Berlin: Duncker und Humblot.

SCHLOTHEIM, H. H. (1965) "Der Laie im Richteramt." Deutsche Richterzeitung 43: 296-297.

Statistical Analysis and Reports Division of the Administrative Office of the U.S. Courts (1982) 1982 Grand and Petit Juror Service in the United States District Courts. Washington, DC: Author.

――― (1980) 1980 Juror Utilization in the United States District Courts. Washington, DC: Author.

Statistisches Bundesamt Wiesbaden (1981) Rechtspflege: Reihe 2.2, Strafgerichte, 1980. Stuttgart und Mainz: W. Kohlhammer GmbH.

STOEVER, W. (1974) "The expendable resource: studies to improve juror utilization." Justice System Journal 1: 39-53.

WERNER, G. (1974) "Die Änderung der Schwurgerichtsverfassung durch das Erste Gesetz zur Reform des Strafverfahrensrechtes: Verbesserung oder Verschlecterung des Strafverfahrens?" Goltdammer's Archiv für Strafrecht, ppl 14-25.

"Why People Complain about Jury Duty" (1973) U.S. News and World Report, December 31.

Peter Wickman

State University of New York at Potsdam

9

ROLE CONFLICT AND STRESS OF
PRISON GUARDS
Organizational and Cross-National Perspectives

Considerable research has been conducted on the social organization
of the prison world in various countries, yet very little attention has
focused on cross-national studies of the problems and well-being of men
and women who work in these institutions. In the United States in recent
years there have been reports of an increasing number of prison workers
filing claims that allege that the constant stress of their work is related
to their being mentally, physically, or socially disabled (Brodsky, 1977:
133). For example, in 1981 the California Department of Corrections
estimated that compensation claims — most of which were related to job
stress — would amount to at least $9 million. California pays disability
retirement funds equal to $12,000 a year for each active guard. Job stress
is also evidenced by high turnover rates, estimated at 50% or more a
year in several prison systems, and as high as 100% in one Illinois prison
(Gardner, 1981: 8; Fogel, 1975: 71).

If stress is inherent in the nature of the prison guard's work environment, it seems important to explore the social organization of that work
environment more fully. It is reassuring to note, then, that in recent years
the number of descriptive studies of the people who play a crucial role
in our prisons has increased. Consequently, it may be more feasible now
than 10 years ago to attempt a kind of composite profile of prison
guards' role expectations and stress factors in their work environment.

Research in the United States, such as that reported by Jacobs and
Retsky (1975), has confirmed the contradictory and dangerous aspect
of the guard's role and has indicated that changing demands have more
or less demoralized guards. While Jacobs and Kraft (1978) have described

tensions between racial groups in the guard ranks, studies by Guenther and Guenther (1976), as well as Crouch and Marquart (1980), have analyzed the socialization of guards by older guards. Jacobs's (1978) data reveal guards' attitudes toward their work, occupation, career, superiors, and other personnel, as well as their perspectives on inmate offenders and criminality. There has been on apparent lack, however, of a conceptual framework that might enable us to relate this accumulating data on attitudes, behavior, and stressful effects of guards' role to the complexity of the prison organization. It seems that sociological studies of prison personnel may have been guided by theories of deviance that traditionally have used the individual as the unit of analysis even in macro-level comparisons of guards' attitudes (Crouch and Alpert, 1980). An exception is Elmer Johnson's (1960) earlier analysis of the problems inherent in the bureaucratic social organization of rehabilitation institutions. To the extent that such studies of prison guards have been informed by an organizational perspective, it would seem that they tend to rely on the rather passé human relations perspective.

My first objective is to emphasize the applicability and relevance of organizational theory to an understanding of occupational stress among prison guards. Second, I will utilize this perspective as the basis for a proposed model to analyze cross-national data relevant to role expectations and stress reactions of prison guards. The proposed model will be used in an exploratory attempt to identify sources of stress (independent variables) and also provide a profile of stress reactions (dependent variables). Our contention is that both sources of work stress and stress reactions might be understood more fully if viewed in relation to the organizational goals, structure, and environment of the prison.

An organizational perspective assumes that organizational factors play an important part in influencing the behavior of individuals—that is, people tend to act collectively in organizations rather than as isolated individuals (Hall, 1977). Three factors pertinent to an understanding of the complexities and contradictions of behavior within the prison organization are (1) organizational goals, (2) organizational structure, and (3) the organizational environment. A brief description of each as it relates to the behavior of personnel in penal organizations provides a backdrop for the model that is used in the presentation of my data.

The organizational goals of penal institutions—as with most organizations—have significance for members to the extent that both official and operative goals reflect societal needs and environmental and internal pressures, identify ends sought, and, in other words, specify what the organization is trying to do in view of its stated purpose (Perrow, 1979). The primary purpose of the prison is to carry out the sentence imposed by the courts (i.e., the main goal of prisons is punishment). The operative goals of this organization might then be summed up as (1) the punishment of convicted offenders, (2) safeguarding society through isolation of some and the deterrence of other potential offenders, and (3) providing services and opportunity within the institution for the possible remediation of offenders.

Analysis of changing prison structures is useful for an understanding of how this social system affects "keepers" as well as the "kept." Early studies of the prison world (Clemmer, 1940; Sykes, 1958), argued that the structure of the prison imposed a deprived status on the inmate who was coerced into developing an accommodative inmate culture. The inmate code and conflict and division between staff and inmates were viewed as evidence of the idea that the prison was a closed monolithic society, an archetype of Goffman's (1961) total institution.

Recent research has moved away from functionalists' interpretation explaining prison behavior in terms of events within the walls. In response to Goffman's (1961) speculation that those who enter total institutions (i.e., prisons) are "stripped" of their former status, Irwin has argued that offenders bring behavioral patterns into prison and that the importation of these patterns comprises the social organization of the prison. Hence, this emergent view of the prison considers not only the internal structure but sociocultural changes and currents in the environments in which they exist.

The prison organization, when viewed in terms of the larger environment, might be envisaged as tied to other social and political institutions as well as having interorganizational linkages with other subsystems of the criminal justice system. Irwin (1980) described the variety of influences from "outside" that affect the prison world. He suggests that the concept "interchange" is a more effective tool for analysis of the impact on the prison world of the rapid pace of social change and related conflict of recent decades. In his more recent work, *Prisons in Turmoil* (1980), Irwin contends that the social order of contemporary prisons are fragmented, tense and more volatile than ever. Nevertheless, he notes that "a high degree of social order still exists even in the most fragmented prisons."

A Model Relating Stress Factors in the
Prison Work Organization to Stress Reactions
of Guards

The model, briefly outlined in this section, will be utilized to confront the problem of the paucity of an integrated perspective relevant to the individual's interaction within his or her work environment. It is adapted from that utilized by Raija Kalimo at the Institute of Occupational Health, Helsinki, for the department of Prisons of the Finnish Ministry of Justice. It was assumed that in general, stress factors in the work environment of prison personnel might be viewed as basic to the organization, managerial style, work content, and human relations within the environment (Kalimo, 1980: 10-11).

I digress to note that although the term "stress" is in common use, no generally accepted meaning is current. Some authors are reluctant to accept the term, but rather consider it a general rubric for a broad area of research. In the operational definitions utilized by Kalimo and his associates, stress refers to an imbalanced relationship between the environment and the individual. The ecological counterpart of this relationship are stress factors, or stressors. The general term "stress reaction" characterizes the response of the individual. "Job satisfaction-dissatisfaction" was regarded as a long-term emotional state — that is, a dependent variable — as was "stress reaction" (1980: 14-27).

The model provides an overview of stress factors or stressors as independent variables. The dependent variable is the stress reaction of the individual guard. The following work stressors are depicted in Figure 9.1 as sources of work stress based on a preliminary analysis of various studies:

(1) *Factors Intrinsic to Task.* These indicate workload variables that do not fit the individual's characteristics.
(2) *Role in the Organization.* This is one of the major means whereby organizational and individual levels of research may be linked (i.e., roles represent the expectations of the organization as viewed by the individual).
(3) *Career Development.* Aspects of this group might reflect work overload or underload, as well as role conflict and ambiguity.
(4) *Relations Within the Organization.* These comprise both vertical and horizontal dimensions and encompass client-oriented work, such as guarding and relations between employees and inmates as well as among employees.

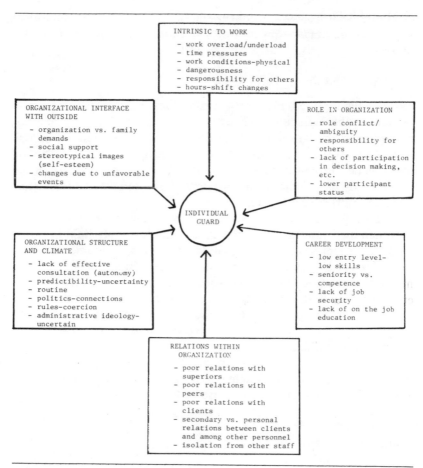

Figure 9.1 Sources of Work Stress for Guards

SOURCE: Adapted from Kalimo (1980: 27).

(5) *Organizational Structure and Climate.* Organizational climate may result from the context (goals, techniques, funding, etc.) and structure (authority system, network linkages).

(6) *Organization Interface with the Outside Environment.* There are certain unplanned adaptations and natural processes in the environment outside the organizational structure that have to be considered [Kalimo, 1980: 23-34].

The model will serve as a conceptual framework for a cross-national analysis of contrasting profiles of role expectations, "stress factors," and "stress reactions," of prison guards.

Operationalization of the Model

The data analyzed will have a twofold emphasis. First, data from results of published studies in North America will be contrasted to information from several studies of prisons in the Nordic countries as well as bits and pieces of data drawn from my interviews with prison staff and inmates. From these data, generalizations will be made for cross-national comparisons (and contrasts) relative to sources of stress (stress factors) in prison work organizations.

This analysis involves some obvious and serious flaws, not the least of which are problems of reliability and validity. Only Kalimo (1980) relied on a representative national sample. Thus, I assume that data reflecting guard's perceptions — the subjective environment — might shed light on more objective potential sources of stress in the work environment. I recognize the hazard of confusing dependent with independent variables, and the more subtle difficulty that the latter may be contaminated by the first since role perceptions and the social structures of formal organizations influence each other in a reciprocal manner. Given these flaws, I make no claims to causality, but view this as an exploratory analysis which might stimulate the search for a more cogent theoretical framework and yield useful hypotheses for further cross-national study.

Work Characteristics as Sources of Stress
for Prison Guards

Data in this section will rely on those provided by the cognitive function of the person as a perceiver of the environment.

(1) Factors intrinsic to work. Studies indicate correlations between the qualities of the guard's work and symptoms of stress. These include subjective evaluations of work characteristics drawn from, inter alia, studies of prison guards in North America and several Nordic countries.

1.1. Relates not only to physical but also mental overload, and conversely, boredom from under-used skills. Data suggest that the United States has the least favorable guard-prisoner ratio of any industrialized nation (Bowker, 1982: 189). Guards are in close and intimate association with inmates throughout the working day—social distance is difficult to maintain and in the eyes of those he controls he is a "hack," a "screw" (Sykes, 1980: 239). Slightly more than one-third of the officers responded that they experienced boredom... most frequently associated with... duty on the...wall or yard (Lombardo, 1981: 139).

Finnish prison guards perceived their work as mentally stressful; over half viewed mental requirements as too heavy while guards... experienced their work as physically heavy... 68 percent responded that work demands increased in recent years... the number of guards were insufficient due to over crowding (Kalimo, 1980: 62). A feature article in a Stockholm (Sweden) newspaper notes that: "the prison guards at Sweden's oldest closed prison were exhausted due to short staff" (EXPRESSEN, November 10, 1962: 1).

1.2. Guenther and Guenther (1980) note: The everyday operations of correctional work, such as locking, making counts, supervising work crews, and delivering mail work against... contact with inmates (p. 163)... serious malfunctions which affect large numbers of inmates demand immediate and decisive attention... (p. 167).

A Swedish guard noted that there were periods when much overtime was accumulated due to small staff and the variety of activities outside the institution (Wickman, 1974).

1.3. Work conditions: e.g., inmate housing facilities are often outdated, overcrowded, or obsolete. Guards may work in surroundings that are noisy and filthy—a hospital built in 1916—housing 150 inmates (Guenther and Guenther, 1980: 166; Gardner, 1981: 10-11).

Common problems reported by Finnish guards were drafty, gloomy, crowded, and impractical (insecure) work places and poor staff facilities. Guards at an experimental Swedish prison felt that custodial aspects were given a low priority (Kalimo, 1980: 62; Landerholm-Ek, 1976: 34).

1.4. Roughly one-third of the Auburn guards referred to danger and mental tension as the "worst thing about the job" (Lombardo, 1981: 115). Custodians... operate in a high stress environment (Johnson, 1977: 264). Danger was listed as the main disadvantage of the job by 49 percent of the guards (Jacobs, 1978: 189-190). Inside the cellhouse of a mega prison guards are at the mercy of the inmates (Jacobs and Retsky, 1975: 16). The guard's world has... come to be pervaded by fear and uncertainty (p. 22). The possibility of trouble always exists... reality shock is experienced by new guards who are tested by inmates (Crouch and Marquart, 1980: 72, 83-84). A guard states, "The inmates had been under constant [Lockup] for almost a year. As a result... their verbal abuse scared the shit out of me" (Jacobs and Retsky, 1975: 22-23). George Jackson's statement aptly sums up stressor and stress reaction: "the days and nights that a guard has to spend... locked in a cellblock with no gun are what destroy anything at all that was good... or social about him. Fear begets fear" (Fogel, 1975: 105). Brodsky (1977) found that... the subject discovered physical or psychological or social dangers to himself of which he had been... unaware earlier (p. 135).

Prisoner threats were perceived as a problem and hostility from prisoners, trouble, contact difficulties, distrust and the need for alertness were ranked high among Kalimo's Finnish respondents (1980: 63, 68). Swedish newspapers reported these perceptions: "Attacks on Guards, but it is part of the job"/"we don't hate, we are afraid" (EXPRESSEN, August 28, 1972). "Murder Conspiracy: Five Guards on Death List" (Dagens Nyheter, December 30, 1972).

1.5. Johnson (1977) notes: "The guard can ill afford to ignore signs of stress... he must actively intervene and provide support and assistance to the crisis prone... until professional care can be obtained" (p. 264). "The correction officer... is functioning as a manager of violent, explosive men but he's not recognized as a manager. He's only a guard, a watcher" (Gardner, 1981: 9).

Finnish prison guards felt the work demanding relative to social and psychological skills, e.g., the ability to cope with inmates; over half reported that responsibility was too high, and the need to respond to inmate demands created pressure (Kalimo, 1980: 62, 68). A Swedish guard referred to need to deal with alcoholic and drug problems of inmates, also that the guards' job involved all the negative things, "like locking up, supervising visitations, etc." (Wickman, 1974f).

1.6. Jobs, most of which are rotated quarterly, may require working in a cellhouse, dining hall, control center, tower, or visiting room (Guenther, 1977: 82). The prison is a 24-hour a day work organization and guards rotate shifts as well as job assignments — shift work has been found to be related to difficulty of fulfilling job expectations, i.e., maintaining a working relationship with inmates (Guenther and Guenther, 1980: 172).

Night work is obligatory in prisons and the average number of night shifts for Finnish personnel during the month preceding the survey was five; 20 percent had done overtime during the past year (Kalimo, 1980: 55). Shift work was reported as an obstacle to participation of guards in an experimental milieu therapy prison (Landerholm-Ek, 1979: 9). The inmates are generally the same group from day to day while guards change. This lack of concentrated work time of guards modifies their effectiveness as 'treaters,' yet the Union seeks to maintain system (Wickman, 1974d, 1974f).

(2) Role in organization. Role stress due to unfavorable linkage between the individual and his or her perceptions of organizational
demands and/or expectations have received considerable attention in
research on work. Reports of different kinds of role stress that correlate
negatively with the guards' satisfaction with their attitudes toward their
work reported in studies on North American and Nordic prison guards
include the following:

2.1. The goals or objectives of the job are contradictory. . . there is role
ambiguity (Brodsky, 1977: 137). As a result of ambiguous and contradictory role definitions, the custodians' pre-existing state of anomie is exacer-
bated (Carroll, 1980: 308-311). . . helping roles which might be played by
custodial staff have not been delineated. . . Guards who act like guards
can disrupt treatment. . . . Officers feel that lack of training, combined
with custodial aspects of their job renders them impotent. . . . Effectiveness in helping is limited in part because they typically receive little
support from treatment staff (Johnson, 1977: 264, 268, 271). Officers feel
it is impossible to enforce regulations adequately (Bowker, 1982: 188).
The officer must resolve conflicts among the diverse requirements of his
role (Guenther, 1977: 81). Jacobs and Retsky note that officers seek to
resolve such role distress by an increased commitment to custodial duties
(1975: 51). Guards at Auburn experienced conflicts in trying to blend
security with their assignments; slightly less than a third indicated they
were bothered by difficulties in reconciliation of these two roles (Lombardo, 1981: 137-138). Sixty percent of Jacobs' respondents (1978)
disagreed with the statement: "rehabilitation programs are a waste of time
and money" (p.192).

Kalimo's (1980) research found that conflicts in work role were negatively
correlated with job satisfaction (p. 73). A Danish prison administrator
noted that guards have a long-standing relationship with treatment which
is a form of control (Wickman, 1974e). In an experimental Swedish prison
the contradiction between the two goals — treatment and custody — were
noted (Landerholm-Ek, 1976: 23). Swedish print media headlined the
guards' dissent: "We are Guards, not Keepers"/"Our Titles have changed
to Keepers, but we still function only as Guards"/"our main responsibility
is still to see that inmates do not escape from prison" (EXPRESSEN,
June 14, 1971; DAGENS NYHETER, June 7, 1971).

2.2. Correctional officers, of course. . . have a great deal of power over
a large number of human beings. The treatment philosophy may have

provided some of the more idealistic line officers with a sense of mission (Duffee, 1980: 206; Jacobs, 1978: 193-194).

"Danish guards have responsibility for treating prisoners" (Wickman, 1974e).

2.3. Concerns among Auburn guards revolved around the theme of powerlessness (i.e., the officer perceived himself as being unable to participate meaningfully in decisions related to the functioning of the institution) — over 60 percent of the guards referred to this at least once (Lombardo, 1981: 113, 120). Yet Jacobs and Crotty contend that collective bargaining agreements have radically changed this (1980: 323-324).

In Danish prisons, guard representatives attend and participate in decision-making staff meetings with representatives of other personnel. In a Swedish prison, due to lack of clarity in the decision making process, guards did not have opportunities to participate, and complained of inadequate influence (Landerholm-Ek, 1976: 9). Focusing on the democratic aspects of the therapeutic community they felt left out compared to inmates in another prison, however, one guard stated: "Guards are more important than a year ago. . . . We have discussions about security, etc." (Wickman, 1974a, 1974f). Swedish print media highlighted progress: "Guards demand institutional democracy for personnel" (DAGENS NYHETER, November 4, 1969). "No Hierarchy, Prison Workers Get More Influence" (DAGENS NYHETER, December 17, 1977).

2.4. Consequently, while he or she is a manager of inmates, the guard is at the bottom of the prison occupational hierarchy. Most officers in Lombardo's study expressed the belief that their work lacked opportunities for recognition — administrators as well as inmates were unappreciative (1981: 123; also see Brodsky, 1977: 137; Stotland, 1980: 295-296).

Guards at experimental prisons compensated for low status, with what the researcher termed "uniform syndrome" (Wickman, 1974a). Swedish guards perceived weaknesses in information and lack of responsibility for decision making (Krantz et al., 1979).

(3) Career development. Certain facets of this may be reflected in dimensions intrinsic to work as well as in role conflict and ambiguity. Research reports relevant to this source of stress include, inter alia, the following:

3.1. The selection and training of guards did little to equip them for their job — the recruit still learns most of his trade by doing it, "I had OJT from a convict"/Entry requirements for guards are minimal. . . . Many states require a high school diploma, yet the minimum in one state (1976) was a fourth-grade education. Except for those with military or police experience, few potential officers have the technical skills needed. Guards continue to be recruited from the lower levels of the work force, and very few have been exposed to higher education (Guenther, 1977: 76; May, 1976: 40, 44; Crouch and Marquart, 1980: 70; Jacobs, 1978: 194). By contrast, in Nordic countries (e.g., in Denmark), a recruit must pass appropriate tests, be interviewed, and begin a two-year probationary period which includes three months of courses (Hawkins, 1980: 56-57). Finland begins basic training on recruitment (in-service); courses for guards have been provided since 1955 for those who choose prison service (Wickman, 1974j). In Sweden new recruits are trained in vocational schools that prepare workers for prisons and mental hospitals. However, they are still recruited mainly from the category of blue-collar workers (Wickman, 1974a, 1974b, 1974f). Old guards reported having reservations relative to the emphasis on aptitude tests, in use since 1966 (EXPRESSEN, February 28, 1971). An earlier news story reported that "a new prison guard began work without one day's instruction" (EXPRESSEN, December 12, 1960). Sweden recruited ex-offenders — a newspaper featured the story of a new guard who had been "inside" 32 times (EXPRESSEN, June 6, 1975).

3.2. Jacobs and Grear (1980) note: "There is a strong belief among guards that you don't get promoted unless you know somebody" (p. 287) Jacobs (1978) found widespread dissatisfaction with the promotional system; seven out of ten guards viewed it as unsatisfactory (pp. 191, 195). Evaluations of job performance was condemned as subjective or political (see 5.4). Consequently, 42% of Jacobs's respondents endorsed seniority as an alternative (p. 191). At Auburn, Lombardo's (1981) subjects felt opportunities for advancement were closed (p. 151). By comparison, in Kalimo's (1980) study of Finnish guards, the possibilities for advancement were also seen lacking (p. 63). In Sweden, guards in the larger prisons can only rise to a certain level; governors (superintendents) are selected from the social services staff (Wickman, 1974f).

3.3. Guard insecurity is engendered by being subject to dismissal if reported ignoring rule violations (Bowker, 1982: 187), although unionization has altered this (Jacobs, 1978: 195; Jacobs and Crotty, 1980: 324). Among Finnish guards, Kalimo found that the most powerful predictor of health status was security in work (1980: 90). Job insecurity was correlated with accident risk, risk due to prisoners, and physical effort. In the experimental Swedish prison the researcher reported a sense of insecurity among guards relative to prisoner advancement as well as a general sense of insecurity relative to the program (Landerholm-Ek, 1976: 23). The deemphasis on penal measures created a concrete type of insecurity, as reported in print: "Discontinued Prisons Are a Shock to Personnel" (DAGENS NYHETER, December 24, 1976).

3.4. *Corrections* magazine's survey of guards in 1976 found young officers expressed the need for on-the-job education, especially in areas of human relations and security skills; the same study notes that most training offered only a "few basics" (May, 1976: 45). Only one out of eight prison systems had training academies in 1977 to provide stress training for all the state's 11,000 officers, and such classes are a regular part of in-service training courses for experienced officers after 6-8 years of service (Hawkins, 1980: 57). Finland provides courses for principal officers who have stayed in the service at least a year. This training is organized to parallel the university B.A. Examination (Wickman, 1974j).

(4) Human relations within the work organization. Relations between individuals — in both horizontal or vertical dimensions — are a possible source of job stress. Interpersonal difficulties may be one source and also lack of relations due to work arrangements. Reports of guard perceptions indicative of these factors include, inter alia, the following:

4.1. Guards, to the prison administration, supervise inmates in terms similar to rules and regulations that govern their relation with those above them in the hierarchy (Wickman, 1980: 536). Consequently, a common theme that pervades many of the studies surveyed relates to poor relations with supervisors (Sandha, 1971; Duffee, 1974; May, 1976; Brodsky, 1977; Guenther, 1977: 83; Jacobs and Grear, 1980; Carroll, 1980; and Lombardo, 1981: 114, 118). Jacobs and Kraft's (1980) recent study, however, suggests that slightly more than half of the guards they surveyed have a positive attitude toward supervision (304-318). Half of the staff in Finnish prisons felt that the attitudes of supervisors towards their well-being was at least somewhat ignorant, and "communication with upper echelons was considered poor" (Kalimo, 1980: 63).

4.2. Conflict between the agencies of reform and custodial staff exist when the professional staff fail to recognize the essentially totalitarian structure of the prison. (Fogel, 1975: 77). In institutions where treatment and custody are prescribed... as coextensive, yet autonomous goals, interest groups [form] whose aim is to enhance their position in the pursuit of one ... of these goals (Maxim, 1977: 383). Conflicting old and new guard lifestyles are reported in Jacobs and Grear (1977, but see 1980) and in Jacobs (1977). Guards circulated stories about the inadequacies of counselors (Webb and Morris, 1978). White male guards in Brodsky's sample were reluctant to have women or minority men hired as guards (1977: 134). In Finland, 27 of the respondents felt that interrelations among staff were tense (Kalimo, 1980: 63). Conflict against guard and social work staff was reported in Sweden as well as conflict against work, foremen and guards (Wickman, 1974a, 1974h, 1974i); also, conflict between old and new — conservative and liberal — guards (1974f). A "radical" Danish guard was critical of fellow guards as well as the administration (Wickman, 1974e). Sexist patterns of Swedish male guards were reported by the first woman guard (EXPRESSEN, March 17, 1973). Several years later guards still reported apprehension about female guards' abilities to fulfill certain duties (e.g., body searches) (EXPRESSEN, March 30, 1977).

4.3. Interaction between guards and inmates is described as a "contest" (Crouch, 1980: 216). Human relations skills may be lacking — some officers were observed handling inmates "in such a condescending or insensitive manner that they created their own problems" (Guenther, 1977: 82). The "stick man" was typified as a guard who "maintains considerable social distance between himself and inmates" (Guenther and Guenther, 1980: 177). A Danish guard referred to inmates in a section occupied by men sentenced for drunk driving as "these criminals"; his "radical" fellow guard suggested that guards were just as guilty of this violation (Wickman, 1974g). Kalimo's study reiterates the social distance that separates guards from inmates (1980: 44). Guards in a Swedish prison were basically non-participatory in a "community meeting" — other staff and inmates vigorously discussed basic changes in policy promulgated at a staff meeting held the previous week; later two members of the inmate Advisory Council, in apparent derision, called attention to a senior guard who was shooting pool in the inmate day room during the meeting, "he has a paper from his doctor which excuses him," they said (Wickman, 1974i).

4.4. Elmer Johnson (1960), in a seminal paper, contended that "the skills and experience possessed by staff members at the lowest status levels of the formal organization," could serve as a "resource for counteracting the formalistic impersonality of the trend toward bureaucracy. . . that impedes resocialization efforts" (p. 356). However, the guards' impersonal stance relevant to inmate problems can result from the custodian's need to deal with role ambiguity (R. Johnson, 1977: 266-267). This is supported by Crouch (1980), although Irwin notes the recent emergence of guards who, due to their similar lifestyles, are inclined to identify with inmates (1977). In his analysis of the Finnish guard's stance, "I only do my job," Kalimo (1980) concludes that this "leads to a secondary relationship with the prisoner" (p. 44). A guard at the "vacation village prison" in Sweden noted the contrast between the intimate, interpersonal relations in that setting with relations at a closed prison where he previously worked (Wickman, 1974e).

4.5. In the study of work stress among Finnish prison personnel one solution to the guard's problem situation was withdrawal to tasks that do not involve continuous contact with inmates or into another place of work

(Kalimo, 1980: 44). Both Johnson (1977) and Carroll (1980) suggest this results from anomie—structural factors—while Lombardo (1981) describes feelings of alienation that are a consequence of such isolation from fellow workers (pp. 113, 121: see also Webb and Morris, 1978: 62-63).

(5) Organizational structure and climate. A given organization may involve a variety of perceived climates. Studies focus on how the culture of the organization affects the well-being of workers, and have demonstrated that "autonomy, self-determination and decision making are important determinants of job stress" (Kalimo, 1980: 33). Reports of guard perceptions relative to such data include the following:

5.1. Among Auburn guards Lombardo found that officers expressed dissatisfaction with the lack of response by the administration to their suggestions, "Thus, many officers refrain from making suggestions.... When they make policy they don't realize what's involved" (1981: 123-124). So the guard faces demands of compliance, yet must make "deals" or cajole inmates into compliance (Sykes, 1980). In Sweden in 1969 guards took their demands for institutional democracy to the newspapers (DAGENS NYHETER, November 4, 1969).

5.2. Occasional references to a convict guard or stick man, those threatened by the absence of repetition and pattern, were noted. Those subscribing to this ideology—about two-thirds of the guards—supported the view that they should expect the worst... and would adopt a style that minimizes uncertainty (Guenther and Guenther, 1980: 174-175). At Auburn one officer reported: "They try to agitate us by always changing our routine" (Lombardo, 1981: 134).

5.3. "The minutiae of the guards" shift comprises counting inmates, signing passes, checking groups of inmates... searching for contraband, or signs of escape attempts. "One day's routine is like the next." "How in the world can you feel worthwhile if you're just opening and closing doors?" "Others point to the heavy burden imposed... by the routine duties of their assignment and the... lack of time for self-fulfilling behaviors" (Sykes, 1980: 238; Jacobs and Retsky, 1975: 14; May, 1976: 47; Lombardo, 1981: 154). Similarly, in Norway, half of the prison guards, in one study, thought routine tasks dominated their work (cited in Kalimo, 1980: 39,44). And 20% of the Finnish guards found work monotonous (p. 62).

5.4. A young officer who does things well but who has political attitudes perceived as too liberal may... often be passed by when promotions are made (Bowker, 1982: 183-184). "There is a strong belief... that 'you can't get stripes unless you know somebody' " (Jacobs and Grear, 1977: 68). "Others. . . believe advancement means politics and a reduction in opportunities to make positive contributions" (Lombardo, 1981: 152).

5.5. Guards have experienced role conflict when institutional rules prohibited their acting in a "more treatment-relevant manner" (Bowker, 1982: 185). An Auburn guard stated, "There's been times I could have done something for a guy, but I couldn't because of the rules." Over 25% of the officers believe that many of the rules they are asked to enforce are unnecessary or out of date (Lombardo, 1981: 90-91). Three prisoners had agreed to and were posing for a picture—a Swedish guard came out and said, "picture taking forbidden." The rule reads: "No pictures without inmates' consent." (Wickman, 1974h).

5.6. In Attica. . . new policies soon led to the decline of the power and status of the guards (Stotland, 1980: 295). Continuing conflicts among the top administrators created a situation of organizational drift. "Nobody knows what we're supposed to do so we don't do anything" (Carroll, 1980: 308). Many officers also experience dissatisfaction with what they perceive as inconsistencies in supervisory direction. "One supervisor tells you one thing and another tells you something different" is a typical expression (Lombardo, 1981: 125-126). In Sweden I was told "the guards tend to be negative towards policy in the experimental prison" (Wickman, 1974a). A social worker stated, "guards think the governor is too liberal, he treats the inmates like boys" (Wickman, 1974i). A newspaper story headlined: "Rules Are Lacking in the Prison System; Insecurity Due to Unclear Statutes" (EXPRESSEN, December 15, 1969).

(6) Organizational interface with outside environment. Variables related to the interplay between the prison guards' work and their interaction with other institutions and their life outside the prison are crucial yet remained relatively unidentified until recent studies (Gardner, 1981). Since the prison social world is involved in a process of interchange with the larger society, it may be assumed that social changes affect the life of the keepers as well as the prisoners (Wickman, 1980: 543; see also Irwin, 1980). Problems in fitting the organizational demands of shift work into family arrangements, social support, and esteem, and the necessity to conform to other than intraorganizational authorities, are noted in recent studies, such as the following:

6.1. "Family problems" was an ambiguous variable in the study of guard dropouts by Jacobs and Grear (1977), yet former guards characterize their wives' fears for their safety as a family responsibility which caused them to quit their job (p. 68). Job concerns do carry over, as one guard's wife noted: "If he comes home a little bit aggravated, then I know he had a bad day" (May, 1976: 11). Those who experience stress cannot always share it so easily: "My wife didn't seem to understand... when I talked to her she was all 'poor boobie' but that's not what I wanted." An officer in New Jersey noted that "some of the guys haven't been on the job for six months and they're already having family problems" (Gardner, 1981: 9-10). An officer at Auburn prison states, "If I take the job home, I get a lot of strain. Six people... that I know got separations or divorces... people I thought were happy" (Lombardo, 1981: 149). Almost a third of the Finnish prison personnel studied and lived on the prison grounds, and most of the respondents would have preferred living outside the immediate surrounding of the prison—far from the prison—and shift work was identified as stress factors for 58% of the guards (Kalimo, 1980: 63).

6.2. A positive evaluation of work is not necessarily related to activities outside work; however, a lack of opportunity for self-development may lead to passivity in fields outside work. Many officers at Auburn indicated that they had developed interests to which they devoted a great deal of time outside of the institution, including involvement in local government, sports activities, while others had second jobs (Lombardo, 1981: 149). Such participation in out-of-work activities and hobbies, however, might be seen as availing one's self of opportunities to obtain social support when needed to counteract any lack of psychological satisfaction from one's work and thus enhance the individual's capacity for an active, self-enhancing life (Kalimo, 1980: 94). Consistent with this view, Lombardo identified only 2 out of 50 guards who were "proud to be officers" and only 6 out of the 50 found the recognition received "most satisfying" (1981: 144-153). Guards feel isolated from the broader society. They call outsiders "civilians" (Webb and Morris, 1978: 62). The recent intrusion of the federal courts into the prison has resulted in changes in policy and the perception that an important social institution guards support in the abstract, is attempting to run the prison. And guards may feel that organizations such as the ACLU, a favorite "whipping boy" which joined with inmate "writ-writers" to obtain the court's support, are outside influences that have undermined their authority to run the prison (Guenther and Guenther, 1980: 173-174; see also Crouch and Alpert, 1980). In Finland, a special supervising board comprised of at least one justice from the Supreme Court visits closed prisons where long-term inmates are held. The Swedish Justice Ombudsman oversees institutions—he received nearly 400 letters from inmates in one year (Wickman, 1974j; 1974c). Charges may be made against a specific guard (e.g., a newspaper reported: "Kumla guard turned in to Justice Ombudsman by 17 inmates") (EXPRESSEN, January 11, 1970). A subsequent headline read, "Kumla guard accuses

Justice Ombudsman of one-sidedness" (EXPRESSEN, February 26, 1970). The guard's organization also had as its whipping boy—KRUM, the organization that sought to humanize and even abolish prisons in the 1970s and was criticized in the press (DAGENS NYHETER, December 28, 1970).

6.3. Guards may be concerned relative to the manner in which their occupational status is devalued: "You have the stereotype from late movies on TV even in this small town... when people find out you're a guard they ask a lot of dumb questions." "A guard is seen as someone who can't do anything else." (Webb and Morris, 1978: 63-65). "Off-duty at a social gathering, where no other guards are present, many may not volunteer where they work." "The idea that I'm just a guard embarrasses me." This is rooted in lack of public acceptance and lack of understanding of what the job is. They concluded: "Even close friends do not know what to make of the prevailing belief that guards are sadistic, corrupt, stupid and incompetent" (May, 1976). However, data from a later study found that only 20% of the guards who dropped out were embarrassed by their work—racial differences were apparent, but still only 37% of the nonwhites reported acknowledged this stigma (Jacobs and Grear, 1977: 66). Kalimo's study noted a perceived lack of appreciation among Finnish guards reflected in comments about the continuous efforts to improve the position of inmates, but not that of the staff; they considered the appreciation shown by society to be insufficient (1980: 63-64). Similar comments were noted in the experimental Swedish prison relative to guards' reactions (Landerholm-Ek, 1976; Wickman, 1974a).

CONCLUSION

Data relevant to the prison guards' perception of their work environment was organized within the model intended as a framework for the analysis of the sources (determinants) of stress reactions and role conflict among prison personnel. This model was based on a body of research findings indicating that human work environments have significant impacts on the manner in which employers function. The limited data, based largely on surveys of guards' attitudes, do not support simplistic solutions. More carefully focused research on organizational aspects of the prison environment is needed so that adequate policy and organizational changes based on an organizational perspective might be identified and pursued. (Gardner, 1981: 12, 13). The model pertains to other service occupations as well. However, the work environment of correctional institutions includes certain singular features; a continuous demand for alertness due to the nature of unwilling clients who rightly perceive guards as a part of the coercive structure, and a wide social distance between the captives and the keepers, combined with an often aggravating social isolation. These have significant effects on workers and may be viewed as sources of stress and related personal problems.

The survey data precluded any assessment of validity or reliability other than of the armchair variety, due to the variety of intentions and variables used in the various studies. It does seem feasible to conclude that stress reactions and role conflicts among prison guards cannot be viewed in terms of any single global pattern. That is, perceptions of guards do not reflect a monolithic profile relative to the determinants set forth in the model. Further studies focusing on various determinants and levels of stress reaction are in order. The accumulation of such data might more fully test the applicability of the model.

Obviously, further research within the framework of developing stress theories, relevant to stressors and stress among prison guards is needed, not only because it is an area slighted by scholars, but because it is a basis for rational change in correctional work organizations. One might contend that penal institutions—in their relations with keepers as well as the kept—should strive for clarity in goals, consistency in management, and a positive social climate. This ideal cannot become a reality given the fragmented and tense social order that now characterizes many of our prisons (Irwin, 1980). Still, necessary organizational changes should be based on a more solid rationale than Brodsky's assertion for developing a balance between prisoners' rights and guard working conditions (1977: 137). Nor should the recognition of stress factors in the system lead to a focus only on the individual—in effect blaming him or her when it is the system that needs to be modified.

By our continued inattention, except for faddish analyses and solutions, we seem to say that somehow prisons, prisoners, and their keepers do not belong to our social reality. Working in a prison is accompanied by an obvious necessity—someone must do the dirty work. But as a job, it may willingly be left to others!

REFERENCES

BOWKER, L. H. (1982) Corrections: The Science and the Art, New York: Macmillan.

BRODSKY, C. M. (1977) "Long-term work stress in teachers and prison guards." Journal of Occupational Medicine 19, 2: 133-138.

CARROLL, L. (1980) "The frustrated hacks," pp. 302-322 in B. M. Crouch (ed.) The Keepers: Prison Guards and Contemporary Corrections. Springfield, IL: Charles C Thomas.

CLEMMER, D. (1958) Prison Community (1940). New York: Holt, Rinehart & Winston.

CROUCH, B. M. (1980a) "The book vs. the boot: two styles of guarding in a southern prison," pp. 207-224 in B. M. Crouch (ed.) The Keepers: Prison Guards and Contemporary Corrections. Springfield, IL: Charles C Thomas.

——— (1980b) "The guard in a changing prison world," pp. 5-48 in B. M. Crouch (ed.) The Keepers: Prison Guards and Contemporary Corrections. Springfield, IL: Charles C Thomas.

——— and G. P. Alpert (1980) "Prison guards' attitudes toward components of the criminal justice system." Criminology 18: 227-236.

CROUCH, B. M. and J. MARQUART (1980) "On becoming a prison guard," pp. 63-109 in B. M. Crouch (ed.) The Keepers: Prison Guards and Contemporary Corrections. Springfield, IL: Charles C Thomas.

DUFFEE, D. (1980) Correctional Management: Change and Control in Correctional Organizations. Englewood Cliffs, NJ: Prentice-Hall.

——— (1974) "The correctional officer subculture and organizational change." Journal of Research in Crime and Delinquency 11, 2: 158-172.

FOGEL, D. (1975) We Are the Living Proof. Cincinnati: Anderson.

GARDNER, R. (1981) "Guard stress." Corrections Magazine 7, 5: 6-14.

GOFFMAN, E. (1961) Asylums. Garden City, NY: Doubleday.

GUENTHER, A. L. (1977) "On prisoner processing: some occupational dimensions of correctional work," pp. 75-85 in M. Riedel and P. A. Vales (eds.) Treating the Offender: Problems and Issues. New York: Praeger.

——— and M. Q. GUENTHER (1976) "Screws vs. thugs," pp. 511-528 in A. L. Guenther (ed.) Criminal Behavior and Social Systems. Chicago: Rand McNally.

HALL, R. J. (1977) Organizations: Structure and Process. Englewood Cliffs, NJ: Prentice-Hall.

HAWKINS, G. (1980) "Correctional officer selection and training" in B. M. Crouch, (ed.) The Keepers: Prison Guards and Contemporary Corrections. Springfield, IL: Charles C Thomas.

IRWIN, J. (1980) Prisons in Turmoil. Boston: Little, Brown.

JACOBS, J. B. (1978) "What prison guards think: a profile of the Illinois force." Crime and Delinquency 24, 2: 185-196.

——— (1977) Stateville: The Penitentiary in Mass Society. Chicago: University of Chicago Press.

——— and N. CROTTY (1978) "Guard unions and the future of prisons. IPE Monograph No. 9. Ithaca, NY: Cornell University, Institute of Public Employment.

JACOBS, J. B. and M. GREAR (1977) "Drop-outs and rejects: analysis of the prison guards' revolving door." Criminal Justice Review 2: 57-70.

JACOBS, J. B. and L. J. KRAFT (1978) "Integrating the keepers: a comparison of black and white prison guards in Illinois." Social Problems 25: 304-318.

JACOBS, J. B. and H. G. RETSKY (1975) "Prison guard." Urban Life 4, 1: 15-29.

JOHNSON, E. (1960) "Bureaucracy in the rehabilitation institution: lower level staff as a treatment resource." Social Forces 38 (May): 355-359.

JOHNSON, R. (1977) "Ameliorating prison stress: some helping roles for custodial personnel." International Journal of Criminology and Penology 5, 3: 263-273.

KALIMO, R. (1980) "Stress in work: conceptual analysis and study on prison personnel." Scandinavian Journal of Work, Environment and Health 6, 3: 9-124.

KRANTZ, L., L. BAGGE, and N. BISHOP (1979) Medinflytande och decentralisering: en studie av organizations forandring pa Kriminalvardanstalten Kumla, Norrköping Kriminalvardstyrelsen, Utrecklingsenheten.

LIPSKY, M. (1980) Street-Level Bureaucracy: Dilemmas of the Individual in Public Services. New York: Russell Sage.

LANDERHOLM-EK, A. C. (1976) On Change in Prison: Shortened (English) Version of the Final Report on an Experiment. Kriminalvardsstyrelsen Report No. 17. Norrköping, Sweden: National Prison and Probation Administration Research and Development Unit.

LOMBARDO, L. (1981) Guards Imprisoned: Correctional Officers at Work. New York: Elsevier.

MAXIM, P. (1976) "Treatment-custody staff conflict in correctional institutions: a reanalysis." Canadian Journal of Criminology and Corrections 18, 4: 379-388.

MAY, E. (1976) "Prison guards in America." Corrections Magazine 2, 6: 3-12.

PERROW, C. (1979) Complex Organizations: A Critical Essay. Glenview, IL: Scott, Foresman.

POOLE, E. D. and R. M. REGOLI (1980) "Role stress, custody orientation of prison guards." Criminology 18 (August): 215-226.

SANDHA, H. S. (1972) "Perceptions of prison guards: a cross-national study of India and Canada." International Review of Modern Sociology 2 (March): 26-32.

STOTLAND, E. (1980) "Self-esteem and violence by guards and state troopers at Attica," pp. 291-302 in B. M. Crouch (ed.) The Keepers: Prison Guards and Contemporary Corrections. Springfield, IL: Charles C Thomas.

SYKES, G. M. (1980) "The defects of total power," pp. 225-247 in B. M. Crouch (ed.) The Keepers: Prison Guards and Contemporary Corrections. Springfield, IL: Charles C Thomas.

— — — (1970) The Society of Captives. New York: Atheneum.

WEBB, G. L. and D. L. MORRIS (1978) Prison Guards: The Culture and Perspective of an Occupational Group. Austin, TX: Coker Books.

WICKMAN, P. (1980) "The dilemma of corrections: treatment, punishment or justice?" pp. 521-552 in P. Wickman and P. Whitten, Criminology: Pespectives on Crime and Criminality. Lexington, MA: D. C. Heath.

— — — (1974a) Interview with Kriminalvardsstyrelsen, [KVS] (Swedish Prison and Probation Admin.) Research Psychologist, C. A. Landerholm-Ek, field notes, August 23.

— — — (1974b) Interview with Lars Bagge, Research Psychologist, R&D Unit, KVS, field notes, August 22.

— — — (1974c) Interview with Justitieombudsman, (Ombudsman for Swedish Justice System), field notes, September 9.

— — — (1974d) Interview with Gunnar Marnell, KVS, Regional Director, field notes, September 27.

— — — (1974e) Interview with guard and inmates at Gruvberget Village, field notes, September 30-October 1.

— — — (1974f) Interview with "young" guard at Visby Prison, Gotland, field notes, November 12.

— — — (1974g) Interview with guard and inmates, Studiegård (Study Prison), field notes, November 11.

— — — (1974h) Interview with inmates, guard, and guard lieutenant, Majorhågen Prison, field notes, November 16.

— — — (1974i) Interviews with inmates, guard, work foreman, and observations, Gävle Prison, field notes, November 19-20.

— — — (1974j) Interview with Head, Finnish Prison System Training Academy, October 29.

SWEDISH NEWSPAPER ARTICLES*

"DET HÄR ÄR INTRE NÅGON LEKSTUGA" EXPRESSEN (August 27, 1972)
"FLER OVERFALL PÅ VÅRDARE: MEN DET HÄR TILL JOBBET" DAGENS NYHETER (June 7, 1971)
"KALLE FANGELSE 32 GANGEN: NUSKA HAN DIT IGEN-SOM VÅRDARE" EXPRESSEN (June 6, 1975)
"FANGARNA INGET PROBLEM för CARINA, 29, forsta KVINNA på MANLIGT FANGISE, KOLLEGERNA ÄR VARST" EXPRESSEN (March 17,1973)
"KUMLAVAKTEN får HJALMAN" DAGENS NYHETER (December 1, 1978)
"INGENHIERARKI: VÅRDARA får MER INFLYTARDE" DAGENS NYHETER (December 17, 1977)
"HUR SKA DET gå MED KRAPPSVISITALIONEN" EXPRESSEN (March 30, 1977)
"INDRGNA ANSTALTER CHOCK för PERSONAL" DAGENS NYHETER (December 24, 1976)
"HAN ÅTERVARDE TILL FÄNGEISET-MEN SOM EN FRI MAN" EXPRESSEN (June 17, 1978)
"KUMLA VÅRDARE JO ANMALS: HAN LÖSER KOR SORDEN FORE OSS" EXPRESSEN (January 25, 1974)
"LÅG BELAGGNING BROAN PERSONAL VID KUMLA" DAGENS NYHETER (November 24, 1974)
"MORDKOMPLOTT FEM VÅRDARE på DOD LISTA" DAGENS NYHETER (November 30, 1972)
"VI HATAR INTE: VI ÄR RADDA!" EXPRESSEN (August 28, 1972)
"VI AR VAKTARE: INTE VÅRDARE" EXPRESSEN (July 14, 1971)
"MAN BEHOVER INTE VARA SOCIONOM för att KINNA PRATA MED KILLARNA" EXPRESSEN (February 28, 1971) pp. 8-9
"FANGVÅRDS PERSONAL KRITSERAN KRUM" DAGENS NYHETER (December 28, 1970)
"KUMLAVARDEN ANKLAGAR JO får ENSIDIGHET" EXPRESSEN (February 26, 1970)
"STADGA SAKNAS INOM FANGVARDEN OSÄKERHET GENOM OKLARA REGLER" EXPRESSEN (December 15, 1969)
"VÅRDARE KRAVEN: ANSTAITS DEMOKRATI for PERSONAL" DAGENS NYHETER (November 4, 1969)
"FANGVÅRD UTAN EN DAYS INSTRUKTION" EXPRESSEN (December 12, 1960)
"LÅNDHOLMS PERSONAL HELT SLUTKÖRD" EXPRESSEN (April 10, 1962)

*Dr. Robert Rose of Stockholm conducted the newspaper archive search and aided in translation.

ABOUT THE AUTHORS

ISRAEL L. BARAK-GLANTZ is Assistant Professor of Sociology at the Wayne State University. He received his Ph.D. in sociology in 1978 at the Ohio State University. Barak's works have been published in sociological and criminological journals including *Sociological Focus, Journal of Criminal Justice, Criminal Justice Review,* and *The Prison Journal.* Barak co-edited *The Mad, the Bad and the Different,* and is coauthor of a forthcoming book, *The Dangerous Offender in Custody.* His current research interests include social organization and management styles of correctional institutions, patterns of prisoner misconduct, and methods of handling long-term prison inmates.

PIERS BEIRNE is Associate Professor of Sociology and Legal Studies at the University of Southern Maine. With Richard Quinney he recently edited and contributed to *Marxism and Law* (1982). He is currently at work on two books: one on the 1920s Soviet legal theorist Piotr Stuchka; the other, *The Concept of Crime,* a text in criminological theory.

FRED HUTCHINGS is currently assigned to the Psychological Services Unit, Metro-Dade Police Department, Miami, Florida. He has been a consultant to various police agencies. He earned a B.S. in administration of justice (1975) at Pennsylvania State University and an M.S., Hiendn Resources Administration (1980), at Bescayne College, Miami. As a Ph.D. candidate at Pennsylvania State University, he is conducting dissertation research on "Community Systems, Planning, and Development."

PHILIP JENKINS is Assistant Professor in Administration of Justice at Pennsylvania State University. He obtained his Ph.D. in history at Clare College, Cambridge in 1978. From 1977 to 1980 he worked with Sir Leon Radzinowicz and Sir Roger Hood as a research officer on their book, *History of the English Criminal Law 1750-1914*. He has published extensively in journals, such as the *Historical Journal, Welsh History Review,* and *Criminology*. In 1983, his book *The Making of a Ruling Class: The Glamorgan Gentry 1640-1790* was published by Cambridge University Press. His current research interests include the history of criminological theory, organized crime, political crime, and terrorism. He is currently engaged in a study of the justice system in Pennsylvania from 1890 to 1940.

ELMER H. JOHNSON is Professor of Sociology and Criminal Justice at the Center for the Study of Crime, Delinquency, and Corrections, Southern Illinois University at Carbondale. He received his Ph.D. in sociology (1950) from the University of Wisconsin at Madison. During his faculty career (1949-1966) at North Carolina State University at Raleigh, he served as assistant director of the North Carolina Department of Prisons while on academic years. His interests are criminological theory, corrections, community aspects of justice policy, and international criminology. His publications include *Crime, Corrections, and Society, Social Problems of Urban Man,* and (editor) *International Handbook of Contemporary Developments in Criminology* (two volumes).

KNOWLTON W. JOHNSON is Associate Professor and Director of Research of the Justice Center at the University of Alaska, Anchorage. He received his Ph.D. in social science from Michigan State University in 1971. His research interests include violence prevention and control, victimology, interorganizational relations, research utilization, and planned change. Dr. Johnson has numerous publications and governmental reports in the police, courts, and corrections areas. Of particular importance has been his recent writing in the area of university-Justice Department policy linkages, "A Change Strategy for Linking the Worlds of Academia and Practice," *Journal of Applied Behavioral Science,* and "Stimulating Evaluation Use by Integrating Academia and Practice," *Knowledge: Creation, Diffusion, Utilization.*

INEKE HAEN MARSHALL is currently Assistant Professor of Criminal Justice at the University of Nebraska at Omaha. She received her master's degree in sociology from Tilburg University, The Netherlands (1972) and her Ph.D. in sociology from Bowling Green State University (1977). She has published articles in *Journal of Criminal Justice, International Journal of Comparative and Applied Criminal Justice, Family and Juvenile Court Journal,* and the *Dutch Journal of Criminology.* Her major research interests are in the areas of juvenile justice and cross-national criminology. She is currently involved in analysis of time-series data on Dutch criminality.

MARIA LOŚ, Associate Professor, Department of Criminology, University of Ottawa, and Adjunct Professor, Institute of Soviet and East European Studies, Carleton University received her Ph.D. from the University of Warsaw (1971). She held academic posts in Poland (University of Warsaw and Polish Academy of Sciences, 1966-1977) and in England (University of Sheffield, 1977-1979). She was a Ford Foundation Fellow in 1973-1974 and has held visiting posts at universities in Oslo, Montreal, and Florence. She has served as a member of the Editorial Advisory Board of *Law and Society Review.* She is the author or coauthor of two books in Polish and two in English (*The Multi-Dimensional Sociology,* 1979, and *Welfare and Justice,* 1982), and 45 articles in English, Polish, German, Italian, Spanish and Japanese. Her current interests include crime and economic crises, corruption and economic crimes in communist countries, and women and crime.

PETER WICKMAN received the Ed.D. (social science) from Michigan State University (1960) and did postdoctoral work in sociology at the New School of Social Research and Emory University. He is Professor of Sociology at the State University of New York at Potsdam. Professor Wickman has published articles dealing with community corrections and penal systems in Scandinavia. Recent books include *Criminology: Perspectives on Crime and Criminality* and *White-Collar and Economic Crime,* which he edited with Tim Dailey. His current research interests focus on citizen involvement in correctional policy and organizations — the interchange effect on personnel and prisoners — and corporate crime.

NANCY TRAVIS WOLFE, who received a Ph.D. from the University of Delaware in 1974, is Assistant Professor in the College of Criminal

Justice of the University of South Carolina, teaching courses in judicial process, court administration, and comparative criminal justice systems. Her projects include an orientation presentation for jurors in South Carolina, a film on the history of punishment in the United States, and articles in *Criminology, Pretrial Services Annual Journal,* and *Criminology Review Yearbook*. Her primary field of research pertains to lay participation in courts, and during the past three years she has investigated the lay judge courts in West Germany, planning an empirical project to be carried out there in 1983-1984.